Mimina

The Slave Girl

One woman's path to freedom

Luisette Kraal

Dedication:

This book is dedicated to women who feel they are still "slaves"— perhaps not to a white master but, nonetheless, slaves to situations that seem inescapable. Be brave, sisters, pray and trust.

God hears your pleas and He will set you free!

God is present.

Acknowledgments

This book is written with the hope that we will all be better informed about the history of slavery as it existed on the island of Curacao, in the Caribbean, and in America.

One of my many 'grandmothers' is the late Suzanna Franciska. She is with the Lord now, but during her lifetime, she taught me many things. When I was signing some papers related to her funeral, I learned that she was born in 1903. That means that she was born only 39 years after Abolition! From her birth date I realized, too, that her grandparents surely would have been slaves! This means that you, reader, could have had great-grandparents who were slaves. How far we have come in the last century!

One of my goals for this book is to shine a light on the daily life of slaves in the 1800s—to illustrate how difficult their reality was, but also to reveal the unwavering faith that some of them possessed, as they persistently prayed that God would see their plight and deliver them.

Some of the painful lessons Mimina had to learn could be lessons that we "free" women of today might also need to learn. I pray God that His love and care for you will shine through the pages of this book and warm your heart.

Thank You

How can I ever thank everyone for all the help I have received over the years with this project? First, I want to thank the writer Dina Veeris for her book *"Van Amandel tot Zjozjoli,"* in which she explains 99 different herbs our foreparents used to heal themselves.

A heartfelt thank you goes to the Public Library of Curacao for their timely help. Also, to my dear college friend Beulah Mercera, who helped me from the beginning, and to historian Lianne Leonora for pre-editing the historical facts in this book. I also want to send a big thank you to my friend Emma Van Delden, who was one of the first people to read *Mimina,* for her helpful advice. Without her, this book could not have been developed.

A thank you goes for Baptist University of the America's (BUA), my beloved college that helped me shape my thoughts into this book, as well as for Moody Theological Seminary, who gave me the tools to divide the Word of God.

In addition, I thank Sylvia Varlack, who has supported my writing ministry from the very beginning. Dennis Rafael edited for me and supplied extra information on the slave Tula. A big thank you goes for my Facebook friend, who volunteered to proofread. Thank you, Ginita Thomas, for editing, proofreading, and coming up with title ideas. My best friend, Jenny Coffi, is, as always, part of this book with her graphic design. Jefcka Alberto agreed to be the "slave" on the cover.

Two other very important persons contributed to this book. Both are with the Lord now, but without their support, I would not have been able to write this book. The first one is Mai Sila, one of my grandmothers. She cared for me many years and showed me all about Mimina, the slave girl keeping chickens and cooking Criollo food. The other person is Papa Bubu from Banda Bou. He used to pass on to me the tales his mother told him about the masters and the life of the free black people living in caves or faraway pockets in the hills of Banda Bou. Much of what I write here is based on his stories.

A thank you to Mr. Elis Juliana for all his books, poems, and stories that I grew up reading. A thank you for Pater Brenneker for his way with words and the proverbs he kept of our history. I thank my dear Texas sister Kim Himnant for being the artist who made the cover come to life! When we were without family in a strange country, she and her friends were family to us, and for that God will shower her with His grace. Also from Texas, Rio Grande Bible Institute is Enid Stanford, my English editor, proofreader, and great encourager. Thank you all so much!

Without all of you, I could not have made this project a reality. Also, we want to thank the organization NAAM and Lida Pandt, who saw this book project and decided to run with it. I thank my many churches: Moody Church (and Hispanic Congregation), First Baptist in Castroville, Iglesia Grasia Abundante from Curacao. And most of all, I thank my lovely husband Ed, and my many children, who were always with me, supporting me, and helping *Mimina* become a reality.

Chapter One

Curaçao, 1827

Didi was twelve the day the Master's wife first saw her on knobby knees, scrubbing the Big House floor. Twelve years she'd been kept hidden. Twelve years living in a stale room behind the Master's plantation house, protected from her Master's eyes. Twelve years her caramel skin had been kept out of sight of those in the Big House.

Mai Sila would have hidden her forever if she could have. But young slaves without skills had only one path laid before them: the fields. Sila couldn't see her child condemned to a life of such back-breaking labor. So, when Didi turned twelve, Mai Sila began sneaking her up the back stairs of the Big House and into empty rooms and bathrooms each morning to teach her the duties of a house slave.

Didi had been scrubbing for hours when *Mefrou* Wilhelmina came upstairs unexpectedly. She stopped to watch Didi making short, quick strokes across the floor with a small rag. Mai Sila froze but recovered in time to bow her head just as *Mefrou* addressed her.

"So this is the child," she began, "... rather scrawny ... but it does appear she has been trained well."

Mai Sila kept her chin tucked and her hands clasped in front of her. "I am happy *Mefrou* approves of her. I am still teaching her."

"Yes," *Mefrou* Wilhelmina continued, more to herself than anyone else. "I suppose she will do fine. As soon as she grows a bit more, I'm sure we'll find a good place for her."

Mai Sila's eyes shot up to her *Mefrou*; a sharp breath forced its way between her teeth. *Mefrou* kept talking, but Sila heard none of it. *A good place ... a good place ... a good place ...* Those three words, *Mimina, the Slave Girl,* set to the rhythm of her pounding heart, echoed instead.

"Sila?" *Mefrou* Wilhelmina demanded. "I asked you what you thought of my plan."

Out of a lifetime of submission, Sila answered, "That sounds good, *Mefrou*. Thank you." She had no idea what she'd agreed to. Only that agreeing was her only choice.

"That settles it then. She'll begin working full time in the house tomorrow. See that she has a proper dress." *Mefrou* Wilhelmina gave a nod, then turned and was gone as quickly as she had appeared.

Sila's hands dropped to her sides. She shuffled backward, slowly, crumbling slightly into the wall behind her. Focusing on the sound of her breathing, she tried to quiet *Mefrou*'s words still throbbing in her ears. Sila understood right away what *Mefrou* was saying. *Finding a good place for her* meant she planned to sell her child. To sell Didi.

With those words, everything in Sila's life became unimportant. Who cared how good they had it here, working in the Big House? Who cared that her daughter was beautiful and light-skinned? With three simple words, Sila had been cruelly reminded that she was, above all else, a slave. Another man's possession. Even after years of subjection to her Master's demands, it was in this moment that she felt helpless. It was this that she feared above all else.

Of course, it made sense. Didi was beautiful, just the right age to bring the highest profit. She was obedient and well on her way to becoming a medicine woman, just like her mother and grandmother, Mai Yeye. Didi already knew how to gather most of the plants used for medications and could effectively treat minor wounds and illnesses for the slaves when her mother and grandmother were unavailable. There was no doubt she would bring a good price.

Sweat slid from Sila's smooth chocolate skin as she fought to contain her grief. She should have thought of this. Should have known. Of course they'd want to sell her. All things considered, it was a miracle she hadn't been sold already, or worse. After all, wasn't that why they'd kept her hidden so long? To keep her out of sight of her Masters, to protect her from harm?

Chapter Two

Curaçao, 1814:

It all had started 13 years ago, with the previous Master and *Mefrou*. Sila was just a child then, serving Master Jan and *Mefrou* Victoria in the town of Punda. She lived there with her mother, Mai Yeye, and her grandmother, Mamawa, both medicine women. It all started in that townhouse when *Mefrou* Victoria learned of her husband's unfaithfulness.

Sila remembered the humiliation she endured during those days. But there was nothing she could have done to prevent it. She was a slave—a house slave, yes, but still at the mercy of her Master. Her own wishes and desires didn't exist as far as he was concerned. She was in this world to serve only his desires. So, when Master Jan called for her to come to his room, she had to obey; when he put his fat hands on her body, to endure.

Despite being powerless to rebuff his vile advances, her shame was complete. She had tried to wrestle him off. She had tried to escape. Each time, his eyes would darken and the beating would begin. It was useless. Her struggle only seemed to excite him more.

The first time she fought him, he slapped her hard in the face and laid a hand over her mouth when she started shrieking.

"You make one more noise and I will call Bomba for you tomorrow," he promised. "Do you understand?" He slapped her again and ripped her only dress from her body. "Do you understand???"

Sila nodded slowly and carefully held herself still. Pain surged through her as he took away what he believed was his from the start. Afterward, Master Jan pushed Sila out of his bed and ordered her to get him coffee and a cigar.

That first night, Sila grew up. She had to. She had been made to understand, for the first time, who she was. No...what she was. She was a slave—usable, expendable, disposable.

When she got back to the small room she shared with her mother, all Sila could do was cry. Mai Yeye tried to help her. She spoke no words, but tried to at least ease her pain. She had no remedy for a broken spirit.

Later that night, Yeye gave Sila a strong, sweet tea to soothe her and help her through the night. And, with the utmost precision, she brewed a more uncommon blend—one meant to prevent Sila from becoming pregnant.

Over the next few months, the abuse continued regularly. Sila hoped to distract the Master by wearing special-day-of-the-month pads (Mai Yeye taught Sila how to lie about those special days). It worked the first few times, but then no more. They tried a number of other methods, but to no avail. Once, Mai Yeye even tried to send Sila away on errands, far from the Big House, but that only made things worse. Master Jan just took it out on Mai Yeye the following day, then on Sila in the night.

Soon, the other slaves heard about Sila in the Master's bed. They made fun of Sila's misery and made up slave songs to the rhythmic tambu, a musical instrument made from leather stretched over an old barrel. The tambu was the most important instrument for making music on the island, used to accompany countless soulful songs about life's troubles. After each day of tireless labor, slaves would gather in "night circles," far from the Big House, and sing and make music. Now, their songs were about a skinny house slave who tried to wiggle herself into her Master's bed:

*Do you think,

because you sleep with him,

you can be lord

over us?*

Sila's days became increasingly miserable, her nights sweaty and disturbed. Her rounding belly began to speak for itself. She tried to keep up with her daily chores, but her swollen middle, puffy feet, and aching back didn't make it easy. She could no longer laugh and carry on as a child. Her playmates, mostly younger slave children from the field, were kept away from her—she was a complete outcast.

And she was lonely.

When Sila didn't have work to do, she would walk around looking for new medicine plants for Mai Yeye. And, all the time, her mind worked.

What will happen if it's a girl? What if she's a white girl?

Sila knew that if it was a girl, she could be sold for a lot of money, especially if she had light skin.

Who would buy such a girl? For what purpose?

She had heard the whispers of her family as they related stories of girls sold at a young age to men-only bars. How most of them were light-skinned.

Finally, her day arrived.

Her water broke early in the morning; Mai Yeye helped her onto a thick mat. Sila spent most of the day tossing, gasping for air after each contraction. The baby did not want to come. *I don't blame it. Who would want to come into this world?*

Sweat rolled from every inch of Sila. After several hours, her eyes had become lifeless and she was not talking anymore. Silently, she wept after each fruitless contraction.

By nightfall, Mai Yeye had begun to cry with her. She knew Sila would die if something didn't happen soon. Her prayers became more anxious.

On the second day, just when the situation was at its worst, Sila felt a cold rush go through her, and the baby made her entrance into the world. Her tiny body was weak; her cry, feeble. But Mai Yeye knew how to take care of small babies. She quickly cleaned the baby's body with her salt ointment and wrapped her in the soft flour-sack clothes that had been prepared long before.

When she finished, Mai Yeye placed her in the curve of Sila's arm. For the first time, Sila saw her child.

And it was love at first sight.

What a perfect creation she was! The pride and joy only a mother can know flowed through Sila. All the pain was forgotten, all the sadness evaporated. She was in a protective bubble, a space filled by only her, her precious little one, and the most amazing love Sila imagined had ever existed.

Sila stroked her child's face gently with the back of her hand. A short laugh, almost a sob, escaped from her when the baby's nuzzling mouth found her breast and started suckling. Somehow, the horror of her memories had faded into another place.

Caught up by a sudden surge of energy—coming from where, she didn't know—Sila straightened, cocked her head up, and spoke in a clear, direct voice:

"Mai Yeye, I will not let my child be a slave. I will not let her endure what I have. I will do whatever it takes to care for my child. I will defend her with my life! I will do whatever it takes ... whatever! I want to be able to raise my own child. I want my child to be a free person. I don't want to be a slave anymore!"

Mai Yeye listened calmly as her daughter spoke. When she'd finished, she placed a hand on either side of Sila's face and said,

"My child. We have been praying for generations that God would see the plight of the slaves. You must trust that God knows and will help us."

Sila strongly doubted God or anyone could help them, but she only nodded and closed her eyes.

Chapter Three

After a few days, Sila was able to return to work. She carried her baby on her back, worked in the kitchen, and helped with the cleaning. She never went upstairs and never saw her Masters. Her baby grew well in those first weeks and continued to gain weight. Mai Yeye did her best to do all the work upstairs in an effort to hide Sila as long as possible. And, for each time *Mefrou* Victoria called for Sila, Mai Yeye had a good excuse prepared for why the child was not in the house.

Sila would be in the slave huts helping out with the children from a young mother that was delivering; in the woods collecting a very important plant; making candles and could not leave the fire. By some stroke of luck, Master and *Mefrou* left for a family party a few weeks after Didi's birth and stayed for thirty days. But, upon arriving home, *Mefrou* Victoria sent for Sila right away.

"Sila. Come here!" she ordered, when Sila was at the door. "Where is the baby?"

Sila hastened to go to her *Mefrou*. With her head bowed and her hands on her back, she stood still and tried not to give any offense.

"Yes, *Mefrou*?" she said. "The baby is sleeping back in my room."

Her voice betrayed no emotion—not a bit of the fear that gripped her—and she tried to speak calmly, hoping to soothe her *Mefrou* with humility and obedience.

But *Mefrou* found fault still.

"So. You think you can be insolent now, just because you have a nigger child?" *Mefrou* spoke in a shrill voice, her face reddening.

The blow Sila received next made her ears ring and her eyes flood with tears. She managed to keep her posture and not show the pain or the hate that she felt.

"Say something!" *Mefrou* screamed and hit Sila again.

Sila thought of Didi wrapped in her blanket in the corner of the kitchen where she'd left her when she came upstairs. Sila had sensed the hostility in her *Mefrou* and knew that her baby wasn't safe.

Struggling to bring normality back to her voice, she said:

"I am sorry, *Mefrou*. Can I serve you in any way, *Mefrou*?"

But *Mefrou*'s eyes were murderous. Mere slits in her pale face. Fear took control of Sila and her ear was still throbbing.

"Serve me? Serve me??? Aren't you serving my husband already?" *Mefrou* Victoria's face twisted in an ugly red spasm. Her eyes were blazing fire, her lips pressed into a straight line.

"I am sorry, *Mefrou*," Sila said hurriedly, trying to placate her *Mefrou* long enough to escape. She kept her face straight and did not show the pain and disgust she felt. But nothing could appease the ire of her *Mefrou* that day.

"And you dare to look at me with that air too?" *Mefrou* Victoria raised her hand in the air, ready to give Sila another blow, but they were both startled by a booming voice at the door before she had time to release:

"What is going on here?" Master Jan thundered.

Both women whirled around. His face was lined from the sun and his hair stood straight up when he yanked off his hat.

Sila watched all the color leave *Mefrou* Victoria's face as she spoke. "This slave is insolent." She tried to make her declaration with authority, but Sila couldn't help noticing how she stammered through the words. "I want you to let Bomba take care of her. She needs to know her place!"

Sila felt her heart drop. She'd had so many beatings already in the months before her pregnancy. Even the tiniest mistake—or assumed fault—and *Mefrou* would call the Fito to give Sila a whipping. When they realized she was carrying a baby, though, the whippings slowed down; probably because a pregnant slave was a valuable property. But most probably because the Fito didn't want to be the one who killed Master Jan's girl.

Sila, at fifteen years, was a slender girl. Her hips weren't very well developed yet, and neither were her breasts, but there was a promise of the tantalizing young woman to come. Her hair was thick and black and fell in soft curls when she let it down, but her mother made sure it was never down. Mai Yeye would weave thick braids then lay them on her head, covering it all with a wrap. She had always tried to protect her daughter from unwanted attention; she knew too well the dangers that existed for a beautiful young house slave.

Yeye was no fool. She noticed her daughter's skin, rich like chocolate; her lips, thick; her eyes, like black diamonds, shining from her face. And Yeye also noticed the field slaves seeing the same things. They were obviously taken with her, even though they knew their chances were slim. A field slave knew not to hope even to hold hands with a house slave, especially one that was also a skilled medicine woman.

And the Fito knew all this as well. He was not going to take the risk of having her beaten by Bomba and possibly killed. Of course, everyone knew *Me-frou* Victoria had reasons to be angry. But, between the two, Fito was more afraid of Master Jan's anger if he let anything happen to his prized possession. That was the reason Fito spoke with *Mefrou* and convinced her to lighten up on Sila's beatings.

It looked like this time, it would be Master Jan who would spare Sila.

Sila kept her chin lowered but lifted her eyes to where he stood in the doorway.

"What is going on here???" he demanded again, his voice filling the room. Master Jan clenched his fists at his side. Sila considered her Master's dilemma. Here was his wife—who provided him with her family name, wealth, and connections—simply aching to inflict as much pain and destruction on the favorite of all his possessions, Sila, whose body he could never seem to stop himself from taking, and who provided the one thing his wife could not: a child.

Sila had heard the other house slaves laughing about how Master Jan had tried for years to make a child with his wife, but, month after month, she had let him down. Then there was Sila, who, within a year of their first encounter, produced his first offspring.

Master Jan swept the sweat from his face with his left palm. Sila noticed his hand was trembling. He was obviously nervous and trying to smooth his hair down, but to the wrong side so that it kept flopping back down in his eyes. Finally, he grunted, switched his eyes to Sila, and began barking orders:

"Go girl! Get to your work! Move! Leave! Now!"

Sila didn't need any more prompting. In fact, she had to slow herself to keep from running from the room. Master Jan slammed the door behind her as soon as she left. She didn't stop to listen to what was said next. She didn't have to. She suspected they were quarreling about the disgusting things Master Jan did to her in the night.

Sila took the stairs leading down to the kitchen two at a time. She was out of breath by the time she reached her Didi, still sleeping in the corner where she'd left her. She hugged her, pressed her tightly against her chest and face.

"Oh, how I love you, small one! You are not his child. You are only mine! And I love you. I will find a way to take you from this place ... I have to! It is too dangerous for you here, my baby. I know she wants to sell us. Or kill us!"

Didi squirmed, trying to free herself from Sila's tight grip. Her chubby arms and legs stiffened in protest. Sila loosened her arms and wiped the tears that had found their way down her own cheeks and had fallen on her child's.

"We have to leave, baby. We have to!"

Mai Yeye came into the kitchen and found Sila, still crying over Didi. She rushed to her daughter, looking her over, searching for a visible sign of what was wrong. Sila tried to turn away and hide the side of her face she knew instinctively would be swollen by now, but she was too late.

Mai Yeye gasped. "What happened, Sila?" she asked. "Was it *Mefrou*? Oh, don't cry anymore, Sila; God will help us. I am sure Didi will have a much better life than we did. Keep the faith, Sila. God will set us free one of these days. Your daughter will be a free woman; you just wait and see."

"Mai Yeye, you never waver in your belief that one day all slaves will be set free. You live your life preparing for the 'Glorious Day,' as you call it; the day you would no longer need to wash dishes; the day you would no longer belong to the Master. You think you have it all planned out. You think we will move— to wherever we want—and we will start a new life, our first real life. But how can I trust God to do this for us? Oh, Mai Yeye, how can you be so trusting? So looking forward for a day that is not coming?"

Mai Yeye pressed her hand softly on her daughter's lips. "Stop talking, child. You don't know what you are talking about. Why can't you believe that God would help us? Why wouldn't you trust Him? Hasn't God helped us until now?" she said in a low, sad voice.

"Helped?" Sila's eyes shot fire. "Helped? Am I free? Could I say 'no' to the Master? Can I move from here and look for another home to serve? How can your so-called loving God allow us to be slaves? I want to be free! I do not think God cares enough to protect me or Didi."

"Oh, Sila, haven't we gone over this many times before?" Mai Yeye tried to hug Sila, who struggled to shake her off.

"I can't just believe, Mai Yeye. I need to do something now. Maybe God does exist; maybe He will help us someday, but I cannot believe something that is written in a big German Bible that no one I know can read. And even if someone could read, we still wouldn't understand it because who speaks German other than some masters?" Tears were streaming down her cheeks.

Finally Mai Yeye could hug her.

"Let's not argue about faith anymore, my child," she said soothingly. "I will keep praying for our family and you will see. God will help us. Do not go tire yourself out with all that planning and hoping."

Sila gave a small nod. But she knew she had to do something. The time for waiting was gone. It was time to do something for themselves; it was time to save themselves.

"We need to leave this house now, Mai Yeye. *Mefrou* Victoria means murder. She will either kill me or sell me—and Didi. I hoped that Master Jan would protect me, but he's in the fields so long, and all day I'm at the mercy of *Mefrou*. You know she detests me and my baby. Why shouldn't she? I think she was hoping to get her hands on Didi today. How long do you really think we can keep Didi in hiding???"

Mai Yeye nodded her agreement. "Yes, I know, *Mefrou* Victoria was very angry today." Mai Yeye's face strained to acknowledge the situation they were in. She bowed her head, almost in shame, then pulled back her head wrap, revealing a painful lump protruding from her scalp.

Sila's eyes grew wide. "*Mefrou* did that to you, Mai Yeye?" she asked, squeezing Didi tight again.

"Yes. She hit me with the stick of the broom I was using. It is true: *Mefrou* Victoria hates us. Our situation is, indeed, not safe."

Sila quickly embraced her mother. "I am so sorry I brought this onto you. Oh, Mama, I'm so sorry." Sila folded over her mother and child, sobbing.

"Hush, child, hush. Just trust God. You have to trust …" Yeye stroked her daughter's back as she continued, "Oh, child of mine; if only I could teach you to trust as easily as I taught you which plant to brew for the summer fever."

Chapter Four

Sila didn't sleep much that night. Her mind raced as she tried to think of ways to escape. She knew from the stories of others how difficult it would be and how often it ended in death. And now, carrying a two-month-old... Sila had no idea where they could hide. She heard of caves in "Banda Bou," as the countryside was called. Would anybody dare to put themselves in danger by telling her? Could she leave the baby behind? Wouldn't it mean sure death for Didi?

Sila pondered the town they lived in. Punda was big. She knew her way around the main roads. She had been there a total of three times with her mother. But to cross town, walk to the woods, and find a cave to hide in—all while carrying a baby?

If only she could find another plantation to serve on, with a master who needed an honorable woman to manage the kitchen and the medicines for the slaves. How many times had she already asked—no, begged—Master Jan to sell her to a house like that? But he refused. He wanted to have her for himself. Even the times he caressed her, stopping to feel the old wounds on her back, he didn't act. He wouldn't sell her.

And Sila could no longer bear it.

She tried to lie still on her mat and begged sleep to release her from the pain. But sleep would not come. She was trapped—trapped in the body of a slave who had to obey her Master's every wish, even the inhumane ones.

Just as the pale rays of dawn finally trickled into her room, a plan began to form in Sila's mind. A dangerous plan, but she knew it could work. It had to. Sila sat up straighter. With a plan this extreme, she could be killed. But wasn't that where she was heading anyway? Sila was desperate. If her plan worked, they would be leaving this house soon. She and her baby. And, she hoped, her mother and grandmother too. There was no other way. Her plan just had to work.

The very next day, Sila began to set the wheels of her plan in motion. She went to sweep the outside patio on the north side of the Big House in the afternoon. She kept busy until she saw Mem walk up. Mem was a slave woman who took care of the piece of land on the north side of the plantation. There Mem cultivated all the plants Mai Yeye needed for her concocts.

Most afternoons, after a day working in the gardens, Mem would bring in a fresh supply of vegetables and medicinal herbs. Today, she carried her big basket slung over her right arm, her left arm draped across its handle. She would have passed right by with only a nod if Sila hadn't called to her:

"Hi, Mem; how was your day?"

Mem's head whipped back, apparently surprised to be spoken to by "that proud house slave." Sila had expected this reaction, but knew Mem couldn't turn down an opportunity to dally and chat.

Actually, it was somewhat surprising that Sila was speaking to Mem. Sila, like the majority of slaves, didn't often interact with Mem—not because Mem was a field slave, but because she was mean. Many of the slaves had received terrible beatings at the hand of their masters, thanks to Mem's knack for spreading news, in her own version, of course. Sila had treated her share of those wounds with Mai Yeye and had heard all the complaints and curses directed toward Mem.

Mai Yeye had instructed Sila to stay away from Mem and, other than polite courtesy, not to have any dealings with her.

But this time, it was all part of Sila's plan.

"Sila, what is the matter?" Mem asked, in a high, false tone. She walked to where Sila stood, broom in hand. "What happened to your face?"

Sila's heart was pounding, but she managed to keep a calm appearance. "Oh, this? It's nothing. It was *Mefrou* Victoria's bad humor. She beats me for no reason, you know."

"Come on, Sila; she does have a good reason to hate you. You have a healthy baby and she is barren. I'm sure it is hard on *Mefrou* too."

"Well, that is not my fault, is it? If *Mefrou* Victoria would take better care of her husband instead of taking her frustrations out on my mother and me, maybe Master Jan would not call for me in the night."

Mem visibly beamed.

Sila knew exactly what would happen now, and she knew her words could easily mean her own death sentence. But she'd had to take that chance. Sila continued, "You know, *Mefrou* must have forgotten that my mother cooks for her..."

She stopped there. That would certainly be enough for Mem to work with.

Mem said a quick goodbye and rushed off to the Big House, undoubtedly to find someone to tell. Sila could just imagine the way her mind would color the story, how she'd tell everyone in the house that Yeye planned to poison the *Mefrou*. Sila snickered to herself as she pictured it all going just as she planned.

In truth, she was terrified. But she had to hold onto the hope that this could actually work. If there was a God, as Mai Yeye claimed, this would certainly be a great time for him to show himself.

Sila knew that Mem would dish up the story with the embellishment that she saw fit. It was time to start preparing for her next step—Master Jan. Around bedtime, Sila made sure she was strategically in the hallway when Master Jan went into his bedroom. Just like she thought he would, he summoned her into his room. Master Jan closed the door quickly behind Sila and started pulling at her dress.

Sila, for this one time, did not oppose him but let him do what he wanted to do. She knew it wouldn't take long with the Master. Quietly, she lay on her back. She kept her eyes tightly closed, like always.

"Oh, please be quick..."

When Master Jan finished, he ordered: "Go get me some coffee, girl. And bring me my tobacco; I left it in my study. All this is your fault—parading in front of me as you do."

He gave her a hard shove.

Sila, waiting for this command, quickly left the Master to do his biddings. Just a couple of minutes later, she came back with the cup of coffee, the tobacco, but also her baby in her hands.

"Here is your coffee, Master," she said while keeping her eyes lowered. "And I brought you our baby too. You haven't seen her yet."

She tried to thrust the baby in his arms, but Master Jan took a step back and refused to hold the baby. The two-month-old baby had filled out nicely. She was peacefully asleep. Master's candlelight shone on her pale skin. Her soft curly black hair looked like her mother's.

Master Jan pushed Sila's hand away. "Get rid of that baby, Sila, you know that it is not mine."

"Master..!" Sila didn't say more. A slave never contradicts her master. She lowered her head. "What would Master like to call this baby? She is one of your slaves now," she said with a trembling voice. She had hoped that the sight of that precious child would have triggered Master's conscience.

Taking a deep breath, she steadied her voice and said, "I called her 'Didi' for now. But she needs an official name."

"I don't care, girl. You can call her whatever you want. You can call her Carmen or Suzanne for all I care. Just make sure you do not call her Victoria. That is the name of my wife."

Sila sensed the hostility coming from Master Jan.

"And do not let me ever hear you claiming this baby to be mine. Take that, that abomination from my sight!"

The Master's breathing was heavy as he spoke. His face was red and the veins on his forehead stood out. Sila could see clearly that he was shaken by the whole thing. And he knew that he was the only one on the plantation that could have produced such a white baby.

Sila was watching him intently, trying to read him, hoping he would relent and save them. For the tiniest part of a second, their eyes met. The Master was the first to look away. But Sila saw his guilt. The expression on the Master's face burned in Sila's head. She understood what he was going through.

The Master resumed his usual pompous behavior.

"Get lost, Sila, I need to sleep. I want you to come back tomorrow night when my wife sleeps. Do not bring that... that... baby... or I will have you whipped."

Sila snapped into attention. This was what she was waiting for. This was her queue. "I might not be here tomorrow night, Master," she said as politely as possible. "*Mefrou* is really angry at me and she has her own plans with me tomorrow, I think."

The Master whirled around, startled.

Sila just stood there with her head bowed while she felt the news settle in the Master's brain. "I think she will have me whipped by the Bomba this time."

Sila heard the Master catch his breath.

"Bomba?"

"Since I am so weak after the birth..." Sila let her sentence hang. She felt more than saw how the words sank into her Master's understanding.

The slave that worked as the Bomba now on the plantations was merciless. He seemed to delight in punishing the slaves. He put them naked on the ground and lashed their back and legs until they were bloody. Usually, the masters from different plantations would let him come only when they needed to punish a serious criminal or a runaway slave. Such a slave would be lucky to survive that kind of beating.

It had happened before that, after a beating, the masters had to take pieces of the slaves' dead bodies and throw them into a dry well. Most slaves had nothing but hatred for Bomba. How could he, being a slave himself, let the masters use him like this?

Sila saw the Master's hand shaking as he drank his cup of coffee. Steadying herself, she plunged into the last part of her speech.

"*Mefrou* has also ordered the Fito to be ready with the carriage for tomorrow. And tomorrow is the slave market day..."

Sila carefully held herself still. She kept her eyes down but managed to peek at her Master to see his reaction. She saw his veins swollen and his face red. His eyes were flaming.

"Leave!" the Master roared.

When Sila didn't obey him quick enough, he shouted again:

"Leave now!"

And she fled the room. Halfway down the stairs, her legs went out from under her and she slid down the steps. She heard the heavy footsteps of the Master thundering to his wife's room, where he entered without knocking.

Then, angry voices.

Chapter Five

Sila ran to the kitchen to find her mother and told her all that happened.

"Child, you have put us in great danger." Mai Yeye wiped her temple and looked concerned. "The whole time this afternoon, Mem was singing a strange tambu. When I heard her drumming that rhythm with her fingers, I got goose bumps all over."

"Which tambu was she singing, Mai Yeye?" Sila asked.

"Bomba call the slave for me," Mai Yeye sang in a low voice, the traditional slave rhythm, the tambu. The melancholic music hung in the narrow hot kitchen. The words were enough to turn their blood into ice. There was not one slave that wanted their master to send for them. And if the Bomba was the messenger, this could only mean grave problems for the slave.

"I'm quite sure Mem was the one who sent for Bomba. That is the only way she could be so smug with all that is happening." Mai Yeye kept looking over her shoulder while she whispered. The sweat dripped from her face and she wiped it off, over and over.

"Start packing some of your things, child; take only the most necessary. Make small bundles. Be quick, girl. Do not stand there. I don't believe *Mefrou* will stand for it that you stay here anymore. Mem is too smug. I think *Mefrou* will have you beaten and sold. Just like what happened last year with that poor boy, Roli's son, from the fields. I only pray that she sells us together."

Mai Yeye's experienced fingers were already going through her herbs. She had a big basket full of small pouches made from washed flour sacks. In each pouch she carried a different herb. Some of her remedies were stored in the hard shell of a dried calabash and covered with a piece of flour sack. Other medications were stored in the square brown bottle previously used for jenever. Mai Yeye was still busy measuring and adding medications and storing them in her sack when Mem walked into the kitchen of the plantation house.

"Is there any coffee left?" she asked, taking liberties.

Mai Yeye didn't look up but kept working on her herbs as if nothing was amiss. "I am not supposed to give you coffee, Mem, and you know that. If there is any left from the pot I made earlier for *Mefrou* you can have it. Please check the pot yourself, I am busy here."

Slowly Mem walked to the corner table while singing under her breath, "Bomba call the slave for me." She poured her coffee into the calabash mug that Mai Yeye made for her, and was slurping it loudly, drumming the rhythm of the tambu on the table.

The tambu rhythm was acknowledged by all slaves as an accepted way of communicating. It was used to sing about their faith in life, about the social situations, but also about their day-to-day quarrels and complaints with each other. Usually the receivers of the rhythmical mocking would just retaliate with their own tambu, telling their side of the story.

Mai Yeye's and Sila's faces didn't reveal the emotions that were boiling inside. Sila started folding some clothes she washed that day for *Mefrou*. She was fuming. And no other tambu came to her mind to counter Mem's song. After this went on for a while, Sila remembered a saying and crooned back:

"When the master gives something away

It is for the Fito that he asks.

It doesn't matter if the bastard is a tyrant,

His soup tastes always good."

Mem looked up sharply. "Are you making fun of me?" she asked with a mean streak in her voice.

"I don't know," Sila said. "If you are a Fito this song is for you, but if you just want to be in his bed it might not be for you."

Sila knew—as did the whole plantation—that Mem had done all in her power to get the Fito's attention. She had made it no secret that she was more than willing to go to his hut at his command.

Mem smiled coldly. "You know, it is because of your mouth that you are in deep trouble right now. Tomorrow we will know who can sing better..." It sounded like a threat.

Mai Yeye looked at Mem and shook her head. Mem's hatred originated from the fact that she wanted to belong to a man. Any man would do. Mem had hoped the Master would summon her into his bedroom. After he chose Sila, Mem wanted to be the one the Fito would take to his hut. She had tried to have a normal relationship before with different men.

First she tried with the slave Dje. He was a slave with an attitude, who ended up on a slave boat to North America to work on a cotton plantation. "They would teach him manners there," the Master said that day.

Then Mem tried with Kun. He was an angry man and regularly Mem had a blue eye or a broken bone. After another episode between the Fito and Kun, he was sold to the plantation Kenepa, at least three hours away. Mem never saw him again and now she was alone.

"Mem, please, take your coffee outside and do not delay my work. I need to iron these clothes for

Mefrou. Tomorrow she goes to the market and she might need them. I don't want to tell her that you made me late."

Mai Yeye looked Mem straight in the face. She saw how Mem tried to hide a smile.

"What are you laughing about, Mem? Do not forget that whatever your Luangu mother taught you back in Africa, my Criollo mother already taught me yesterday," Mai Yeye said.

Mem's eyes shot wide open and she clenched her hands. She spun around angrily and stalked toward the door. There was no way anybody would let her forget that she came on a ship from Africa while the rest of the slaves were born from Criollo slaves.

"We will see tomorrow who knows more," she promised as she left in a huff. Outside, the women could still hear her singing, "Bomba call the slave for me."

As soon as Mem left the kitchen, the women dropped their lazy movements and in a frenzy started preparing. Mai Yeye went to their room to awaken Mamawa, Sila's grandmother. In these days Mamawa, who was very old and bent over, would take to her bed early after dinner and would not come out again until the next morning.

Mamawa was the only grandmother Sila knew, even though she was not related to them by blood. Mamawa could remember many slave ships arriving on Curaçao. She knew many masters. In fact, she had produced eight sons for them; and all eight had been sold by those same masters. Some of her sons died when they took part in the rebellion under the leadership of the hero slave Tula. There was a small chance that one of Mamawa's sons had escaped and lived in the caves in Banda Bou, far from civilization. Mamawa prayed faithfully for him. She was not bitter because her boys had died for the cause of setting the slaves free. She had stated that she would rather have had dead sons for that good cause than slave sons for her masters. In death they were free in the Lord anyway, Mamawa believed.

When Mai Yeye was born, she was premature, and Mamawa had saved her from almost certain death. Nobody else was interested in the skinny, sickly child whose mother died while giving birth, so Mamawa was allowed to keep the baby. She nursed her to health, making sure to teach Yeye how to become a skilled medicine woman who would be valuable to her masters.

Mamawa knew a lot about God. She learned all about faith in Africa when a missionary came to live near the Gold Coast. After her father and the whole tribe attended his prayer meetings, God had changed all their lives and they began serving Him. But one day their village was raided and Mamawa was sold into slavery. She was forced to walk for weeks at a time until they reached a boat to transport them to the Caribbean. She never saw her family again, but never forgetting all that she had learned, she passed it on to Yeye and later to Sila, her adopted family.

When Mamawa spoke with God, it was as if she were speaking with a living person that you could actually see. And although she could not read nor write, her faith in the God of the Bible never wavered.

Mai Yeye and Sila depended on Mamawa's faith and prayers. As soon as Mai Yeye briefed Mamawa about what was going on that night, Mamawa started praying.

Sleep did not come to Yeye that night, as she sat in her chair and prayed.

Sila lay down on her mat and tossed and turned the whole night. She slept on and off between horrible nightmares about what would happen to her daughter and her family. Now, as the hours passed, she worried about what she had done and began to wonder if she should have done it. The urge to pray was strong but she resisted it. Religion was for the weak. She took matters into her own hands. She was going to save her daughter from *Mefrou*. This was the only way she could have done it. She was certain, but still...

Would it work? Now that the Master had seen the baby, the only baby he had, would he do something to rescue her? Would he care enough about a slave's child? Around and around in her mind, the questions whirled. She kept looking at the only small window in their room, waiting for the pale sky to announce a new day.

Long before it was morning she gave up any hope for sleep and opened her eyes and sat up. She was alone in the room. She carried clean water from the well, washed herself thoroughly, and put on her only clean dress. "Whatever happens with me today, let it happen with a clean dress," she thought as she was tempted to smile.

She carried Didi to the big kitchen and joined her mother and grandmother there. Everything was dark. Mai Yeye was still trying to get a fire going.

In this quiet, early morning darkness, they heard stealthy footsteps approaching the kitchen. The three stared at the door and, to their dismay, they saw the handle moving down... slowly. Little by little, the door was pushed open; Sila shrieked and held her mother's hand tight. Mamawa prayed under her breath. Mai Yeye's eyes were glued on the door. She held a broomstick in her hand, ready for what-ever or whoever would come.

Suddenly, Master Jan was standing in the dim light of the fire.

"Master!" Sila cried and swooned.

Chapter Six

None of their masters had ever been in that small, hot kitchen. They just rang the bell and expected to be served promptly.

The Master put his finger in front of his lips. "Shhhh, be still. Take the child and follow me. I have transportation for you."

As he spoke, he pulled firmly at Sila's arm. When she hesitated too long, he said, "Quick, lazy girl. Be quick before ..." He didn't finish his sentence—didn't need to—the words hung in the air.

Sila nodded. She understood and swiftly gathered her bundle of belongings and her baby. "I cannot go without my mother, Master; she takes care of the baby for me and helps me when I need to work.

I wouldn't know how to take care of the baby."

Master Jan squirmed, and his eyes turned red as he pulled harder at Sila's arm. "You go with me! Do you want to stay and die?"

"I am going too, Master; I don't want to die either."

Mai Yeye spoke those words with the authority of a black woman used to giving orders in her sick room. Her tone was the same one she used to speak to one of the field slaves who took too many liberties in her kitchen, not her normal tone when addressing her Master. For the first time in her life she looked her Master square in the face. Then, slowly, she lowered her eyes and tried to assume the slave posture.

Obviously Master Jan had not expected this complication. "Let's go then," he grunted angrily. "It will be light shortly and I want you out of here."

When they started toward the door, the elderly Mamawa, stooped as she was, also began shuffling in that direction. She was wearing her only good dress, and on the top of her head, she already had fastened her bundle. "I am going too, Master," she affirmed matter-of-factly.

The Master almost exploded. He pulled Sila and roughly tried to carry her off to the waiting carriage. But Sila struggled and held onto her mother, who had her arms around Mamawa.

Mamawa interfered with a clear voice. "Master, I have worked my whole life. I took care of children, cooked, washed and cleaned. Now I am old. My fingers are crooked, and I cannot work anymore. These women are my family. Who is going to take care of me when they are gone? Have mercy on me, Master. Wherever you send them, send me."

Master Jan, with blazing eyes and a puffy red face, stood still and looked them over. Now that the women had stated their wishes, all three stood in the perfect slave position with bowed head and total submission to their Master. He was not fooled by them. He accepted defeat. Gruffly, he commanded them to get into the carriage. "For heaven's sake, be quick and quiet."

The women did not have time to enjoy their first victory over their Master. They had dared to demand something and lived to receive it. Although fearful of the unknown, the women hastily shuffled to the carriage. Even the horses moved nervously in the darkness of the early morning.

"Where are we going?" Sila had the courage to ask.

"Get in and do not waste time," the Master barked as he slapped her with a sweaty hand.

Quickly, all three of them climbed into the carriage. The driver was the Fito from the country plantation.

It was not Bomba ...

****

Even before the women were well seated, the horses started off with a fast walk. It was still dark outside. Sila was quiet as she peered through the window. She never knew that the town of Punda was so large. She tried to follow the path they were taking but quickly was confused. She closed her eyes and for one second pretended to be on a pleasure drive. For a short moment she was peaceful. The Master had done something to save her. Her plan worked.

With tears in her eyes, Sila grabbed her mother's hand and squeezed it. Mai Yeye's face was also wet with tears, and when they looked over at Mamawa, so was hers. All three held hands and quietly reflected on what had already happened today and what the rest of the day might bring. They were out of the Town House, but where would they be tomorrow?

Mamawa sat with closed eyes, her lips moving in a silent prayer. Mai Yeye helped every time the baby cried, but her words were few.

The horses speedily took them farther and farther from the Town House and from the vengeance of *Mefrou* Victoria. The carriage continued to move quickly until they arrived at a big crossing. More vehicles were coming and going. The pale sunrays announced the day and people on the carriages noisily greeted one another. After a brief stop at an intersection, their rig turned to the right and sped away.

Mamawa's and Mai Yeye's eyes met, and they burst into laughter.

"What's going on?" Sila looked bewildered.

The two older women were carried away with joy. They kept laughing, clapping their hands, trying to speak, yet laughing again.

Mai Yeye, meanwhile, hugged Sila and squeezed the baby. When she regained her composure, she said, "Child, the slave market is to the left. See? That was the turn to Zuurzak. We passed it and we are driving away from it. So the Master is not going to sell us on the market. If he did, we would not have been sold together. Master has another plan for us. Thank you Lord! That it will be your plan," Mai Yeye enthused.

For this one time, Sila almost agreed with her to give thanks to the Lord. "Are you sure, Mai Yeye?" she asked.

Mai Yeye nodded. "God bless him for not bringing us to the market! How humiliating it is when people open your mouth to look inside to see how your teeth are. How much more humiliating when they rip your clothes from you to see your breasts and the rest of your body. Who knows who would have bought you, child? It could have been someone worse than Master Jan. I hope he sells us to a good clean family."

"Yes, God, guide him and let his relationship with his wife be restored," Mamawa prayed out loud.

Sila's head shot up and she said sharply, "He knows what he did. I will not pray for him. He denied Didi but he knows the truth. I hope his wife leaves him and her family strips him. I hope he dies. I..."

Sila was going to say more but her shocked mother placed her hand firmly over her mouth, preventing more hatred from spewing out.

"Do never speak like that, child. Do not let bitterness take root in your heart. Do never let hatred take over. You might end up just like them. Do not get revenge other than with prayer. God will take care of them. Just wait and see."

Sila let the words of her mother—which she had heard many times—hush her, but in her heart she didn't have the patience to wait on God.

Deep in their own thoughts, the women fell silent again. They were weary and slumbering, only to be rudely awakened when the carriage fell into a deep crack in the street. Baby Didi cried fearfully. Suddenly the carriage stopped. When they looked outside, they saw a coffee house.

The Master walked around the carriage and barked, "Shut that child up before I do it!" He then strode to the coffee shop, leaving Fito with the women. Fito made sure he stayed close enough to supervise them but far enough not to be involved with them. Whatever their disaster was, he did not want to be part of it.

He took the horses to the stable next to the coffee shop, gave them water and brushed them down while keeping the women in sight.

Sila's body was stiff when she tried to sit down on the curb. She noticed Mai Yeye and Mamawa were feeling the same way. Nobody talked.

Mai Yeye helped Sila unwrap the crying Didi so she could get some fresh air. The baby nursed after Mai Yeye changed the flour-sack-rag her diaper was made of. They used the shawl to loosely drape it over Sila to cover her. All three of them wished they had remembered to bring something to eat, but none had. The sun was already hot and they were thirsty.

Nobody complained. Since when did complaining help any slave?

After some time, Fito brought them a piece of his pancake and one mouthful of coffee for each. Gratefully they accepted it.

Shortly after that, the Master emerged from the coffee bar and they resumed their trip.

It dawned on Sila that the island of Curaçao was bigger than she had thought. It appeared that the Master was bringing them to a country plantation, for the streets were definitely not city streets anymore, and the houses were far apart.

The women slept a little as the trip continued. After another hour of travel they stopped again. They were now in front of a spacious plantation with yellow walls and a red roof. The plantation house was surrounded by green plants, some of which were in big pots; others grew on the pillars and displayed white and pink flowers. Leading up to the majestic front doors was a grand, broad set of steps.

Sila saw the two women who were watering the plants give a polite nod to the Master when he walked up the steps to the front door. Every aspect of that plantation house was tidy and well cared for.

The medicine women huddled closely together and intently followed the Master's every move as he knocked on the front door. Immediately, a round black lady opened the door and ushered him inside.

Sila was trembling. She held tightly to her mother and grandmother. Her ears were drumming from all the noise inside her head. Will this be the place? Will the Master really sell them to this plantation?

At that moment the Master appeared in the front door and signaled Fito to bring the women in. Quickly Fito helped them from the carriage and around the big structure to enter through the kitchen door. A slave never enters a white man's house by the front door. Through the kitchen they were led to the sitting room.

They stood there, with their backs close to the wall, in the position fitting for a slave and waited to learn of their fate. The Master sat in a comfortable chair facing the window. The motherly looking slave who had opened the front door brought him a cup of coffee while he was waiting for the Master of the home to come from the fields.

Master Jan drank his coffee without one word to his slaves. They remained standing next to the door, waiting for their future to be revealed.

A noise at the door announced the arrival of the Master of the house. Master Pe came in, still dusty from the fields, with some hay stalks peeking out of his hair.

"Jan!" He bellowed. "So you brought me the slave that I need for my mother? That is nice of you." But at that moment he spotted the three adult slaves standing in his sitting room, one of them holding a baby. He was visibly confused. "What are they doing here?" he asked. "Who are they? I was expecting just one slave girl."

"Pe, I brought three women for you. I would be much obliged to you if you could take all three off my hands. You will see how well they will take care of your house, the kitchen and any sick slaves. Keep them together because they are good medicine women. Wherever you were going to put the one, put the other two together."

Master Pe looked the old Mamawa over. Clearly he doubted his friend's judgment in this.

Hurriedly Master Jan assured him, "She is amazing with herbs. Give her any herb and she makes medicine out of it. She can make concoctions for almost any ailment. And the young one goes into the woods and collects the leaves. The mother is also a medicine woman who can cook very well. Just try them out and you will see."

Master Pe knew that Jan was a powerful man in town. If he could get three medicine women and have a grateful Jan in his debt, he would not refuse.

"Sara, take these women to the place you pre-pared for them."

And to the three women he said with a cool, but not unkind, voice, "If you obey the rules of this house you will live well here. Go now and get started with your work. We do not like lazy slaves on this plantation."

A flustered Sara promptly obeyed her Master and maneuvered her collection of women slaves back to the kitchen. She saw how Mai Yeye helped Mamawa manage the stairs. In the kitchen she offered them a cup of coffee and some porridge. With grateful hearts, the women sat down and accepted the food.

The lumpy porridge was definitively too sweet, but the women didn't say anything. Mai Yeye complimented Sara on the space in the kitchen. It was so large that a whole dining table fitted in it. Sara beamed, obviously proud of her kitchen.

"How come Master Jan brought all four of you here?" she asked curiously.

Mai Yeye didn't want to go there, so instead she just introduced her family. "This is Mamawa; she came from the slave boat a long time ago. She is like our grandmother and we take care of her and all her needs. She is an excellent medicine woman. This is Sila my daughter with her daughter Didi. She can work in the kitchen, house or with medicine. My name is Mai Yeye and I can work with you in the kitchen if the work is too much for you or I can do whatever you tell me to do. We know this is your kitchen and your house so you just tell us what you want us to do and we will do it."

Sara's eyes brightened, as did her smile.

Sila saw her reaction and understood. Of course Sara had been afraid when she first saw them and realized that they would be living and serving in the Big House. Light-skinned, Criollo-born slaves could be very hard on the black African slaves, looking down on them and treating them with hostility.

"How long have you been working on this plantation?" Mai Yeye asked cordially.

"I don't know, but it has been a long time. Before I lived here I lived with another master in town. My job was to have babies. I had twelve babies since I came from Africa on a boat. When I stopped having babies my last master sold me on the market. Master Pe bought me there. I was too old for babies but he didn't need babies. He just needed a woman to clean this big house. Since I came to live with this master my life has been much better," Sara said.

"I was only a cleaning woman when I arrived but now that we don't have a cook or someone to take care of the Master's old mother, I do all those chores too."

Sara looked at the empty porridge bowls and said, "Come on, now. I will show you your place and then you need to come back to the kitchen and start helping me. You heard what the Master said."

Chapter Seven

Sara led them a few steps behind the Big House into a small one-room space. There was one mat on the floor and next to it, one box to hold some personal items. That was all the furniture in the room. Clearly they were not expecting three grownups and a baby.

"Do you need anything for the baby?" Sara asked kindly. When Sila declined, she continued, "I will go see if I can find Bobo to come help you get settled. You will need two more mats for tonight or at least some straw."

On the short walk to and from the Big House, Mai Yeye looked around with great interest. There was not much time to contemplate their surroundings, but what she saw looked promising.

After they dropped their bundles in the tiny room, Sara took them right back to the kitchen. Mamawa took a seat at the long table, organizing her herbs.

Mai Yeye took over the cooking from a relieved Sara. Sila nursed the baby before starting to wash the dishes. They kept up a steady stream of small talk. As soon as the house bell summoned Sara to the needs of the Master upstairs in the Big House, the women were alone to talk privately again.

"Praise God," Mamawa said. "Look what God has done for us again! We are in a big new kitchen. We were sold together. We can keep the baby. Sila, do you still doubt your God?" Mamawa moved painfully from her seat to the water bucket and started washing some leaves.

Mai Yeye joined in the praise. "Our God did it again for us. Now you need to believe, child."

Sila grinned from ear to ear. "It is a miracle, isn't it? It worked. Master Jan finally did the honest thing." Sila walked to Mamawa and took the plants from her. "I wish you could rest a little on the mat in our room, Mamawa, I can do this for you."

She tried to take the pouches away from Mamawa, but Mamawa held on. "Child," she said, "when I was younger I used to travel around all the time. My master would hire me out to plantations that did not have a medicine woman. When your mother Yeye was a young child I used to take her, and later she went all by herself. We used to go to Zuurzak to take care of sick slaves when they arrived on the slave ships. Do you know how many sick slaves we treated from those ships? They had infections, suffered from fevers, vomiting, and had open wounds."

Mai Yeye nodded her head in approval. "Remember, Mamawa, how we made tea after tea to help the poor people get back on their feet? It is a pity their master sold them afterwards as slaves." Mai Yeye shook her head.

"How could you speak with all the different people, Mai Yeye? Didn't they come from all over Africa?" Sila asked while she was drying the leaves.

"I was good with languages. I spoke with people from Kosta di oro, Elmina, Fida, Ardra, Accra, Bercou, Angola, and Luango. I learned to understand their language and help them. That is actually how I met Mem."

"Wicked Mem, you mean," Sila murmured.

For this one time Mai Yeye didn't reprimand Sila about the name-calling. "She sure forgot quickly how weak she was when they dragged her from that boat. She had ulcers, was covered with dirt and fleas. I cleaned her up, sat for hours with her and fed her small amounts of thick chicken soup. And when she was healed I asked *Mefrou* to buy her so I could help her. She was so slow to learn. If it was not for our *Mefrou* she would have been sent to the salt plantation," Mai Yeye said. "How is it possible that Mem could have forgotten?"

Sila shook her head too, but suddenly she burst into a loud laugh. "Bomba call the slave for me... only... there is no slave to call this morning."

Mamawa and Yeye joined in the laughter.

Sara found them like that. "Happy slaves makes good slaves," she quoted her *Mefrou* jokingly. They all laughed again.

Sara walked over to Mamawa to check out the herbs. Mamawa showed her some of them and explained their general use.

"So you all three are really medicine women?" she inquired, surprised.

"Yes, Sara," Mamawa explained. "You can send all sick slaves to me or to Mai Yeye. We will take good care of them. Sila can help you serve the table, wash the clothes, help in the kitchen, or she helps us with preparing and administering the medicine. We taught Sila all that we know, and as she keeps growing she will be using this knowledge."

"Is this a calabash?" Sara asked, shaking a round green fruit containing a liquid.

"Yes, I use the calabash shell. I make holes in it and dry it out," replied Mamawa. "Then I pour the medicine in it. See? I close it with a small piece of calabash wood that fits tightly."

"What kind of medicine do you make with calabash, Mamawa?" Sara asked.

"I can use the fruit for many medicines. I treat people with skin problems with an ointment I make out of it. I use it to make a compress for bruises or pain. It is not only good for the skin but also to make juices and syrup. The juice reduces fever; the syrup

I give to people that cough. I cook it with part of the calabash wood then. I can also make tea out of the leaves. They help to regulate the heart, and if a baby doesn't want to come I give the expecting mother calabash. It helps always," Mamawa said.

And Mai Yeye added with a smile, "I saw some good calabash trees right in the woods behind our house. Some of them have calabash fruit growing. I could use their hard shells to make us some nice cups for water and for coffee. I could make a kèlèm-bè, a spoon to eat our soup or to cook with. I can even make a small toy for Didi with a small calabash. And with the seed you can make medicine, Mamawa. Sila can cook them up for you. Can't you, Sila?" Mai Yeye turned and looked at her daughter.

"Yes, Mai Yeye, I can cook them. I saw those trees too. They look wonderful. And I saw a big stump of an old tree not far inside the woods. If we can get one of the boys to help me roll it over, we can work on it and make a nice table. What do you think, Mai? We can put it in this corner so we can have a place for our cups and bowls."

"It was a good day when we arrived at this plantation," Mai Yeye surmised. "It is rich in all that we need to make us a good living."

"And we are together," Mamawa said. "For now this is the best we have; let's make good use of it and help raise that child of yours in the Lord's way," she advised, smiling at Sila. "We need to teach her medicine and the use of herbs too. For she might be the generation that will be free of slavery. I want her to be prepared to work as a free medicine woman."

"*Mefrou* will be happy with your skills. We really need more help on the plantation. You and Yeye can do that while Sila will be the caregiver of *Mefrou* Jana," Sara smiled.

****

In the following days, Mai Yeye, Sila, and Mamawa quickly adjusted to their new environment. Didi didn't mind the changes in her life. She was quite satisfied if one of her many mothers tended to her basic needs.

Mai Yeye worked hard to make their room livable. The first nights they slept on straw, but soon after that, Mai Yeye made a comfortable mattress for Mamawa and then one for herself. Close to their room there was a well, and Sila was sent early in the morning to fetch water.

"Thank you, Lord," Mai Yeye said in a high voice full of praise when Sila came back and they all washed up. "I panicked for a moment in the house of Master Jan, but YOU were in control and knew all along about this plantation. I see so much potential on this plantation. Our family will live well here. Thank you for taking care of us, Lord."

Sila was introduced to her responsibilities. She learned readily because the work was the same as it had been in the Town House of Master Jan. Sila joined in the cleaning, washing, and preparing of the meals for the family, working next to Sara.

"Sila," said Sara, "you were bought to serve the mother of our Master. Her name is *Mefrou* Jana. She lives upstairs and needs somebody to attend her. Her last slave—who had been with her for years—died, and it was difficult for the Master to find a good woman to take care of *Mefrou* Jana. Good slaves are never for sale. Most good women slaves are not sold on the market. And *Mefrou* Jana needs somebody that knows about taking care of a patient."

"I can help you with that for sure, Sara. I have a lot of experience with sick people."

"I heard *Mefrou* say how happy she was that you know about patients. She was afraid that she would get somebody straight from the boat. But you will do fine. What do you think of our *Mefrou*?"

"She looks nice enough to me," said Sila without committing herself. "I am more concerned for the Master than for his wife. I hope he is nothing like our last Master Jan."

"I know about bad masters," Sara said with a sigh. "I have had a share of them. I was stolen from my family in Africa and sold to a cruel master. We marched for days, shackled together and with almost no food. Then we were sold again to a sea captain. There were more women on board because there was a need for women in America, to breed more babies. But the conditions on board the ship were—some of the women died right away."

Sara shuddered when she remembered her trip from Africa to the Caribbean. "Some of the women went crazy or fell in a stupor. The reason I survived it was because I had a blackout. The only thing I know about this voyage was that I arrived pregnant. I had a baby boy. He is long sold to a ship going to America. I never heard anything more from him. But after him I had many more babies. For the masters..."

Sila and Sara stood still and looked at each other for a second. One more time, Sila realized that she had been much better off than many other slaves.

"Oh Sara," she sympathized. "I am so sorry."

"You will find these Masters to be easy to please. If you just do the work and stay as much as possible in the background, you will do fine. They want us to serve them, but they don't want to see or hear us too much. They will treat you well if they are happy with your work."

"I am sure we can do the work, Sara. We used to run the whole Town House for *Mefrou* Victoria in Punda with lots of people coming and going all the time. Many visitors stayed over. Master Jan had important businesses."

"I am happy with your family coming to live with us. This plantation is just too big for just me and the day help. I am not a good cook, and I certainly cannot help *Mefrou* Jana like she needs. She always ends up screaming at me or throwing things. You are young and you know a lot. I am sure Mamawa will help you if you have questions. Yes, I am happy you are here," Sara said, smiling broadly.

That morning they worked hard, carrying water for the house, cleaning the slop, cleaning the breakfast room, and preparing the table. By the time the family gathered for their breakfast, the slaves had hours of work behind them already.

Sila was supposed to serve at the table, but she was self-conscious about it. She wore her oldest dress and had her hair tight under a wrap. "I really hope Master Pe is not like Master Jan," she thought for the hundredth time that day.

As soon as Master Pe entered the room, she tried to get a good look at him. He was an older man, slender and tall. His face was withered from the sun, and his hair grew around a large bald spot on his head. His hat was tilted up, but he took it off when he sat down. Around his neck he wore a red wrap, probably to protect from the sun and to catch perspiration.

Shortly after he entered, his wife, *Mefrou* Jo, came in. She didn't acknowledge the slaves. She was dressed for a formal affair in a red shiny material that Sila had never seen before. It fitted snugly around her slender body. Her long blonde hair had been brushed by Sara that morning until it shone. Then Sara made long braids that she carefully laid in a perfect circle on *Mefrou*'s head.

Mefrou had penetrating blue eyes. They were not unkind eyes, but rather matter-of-fact. She stated her wishes and expected everything to run smoothly. She wanted to be served rapidly. She received a lot of visitors and hosted enough tea parties to keep herself busy. She had no time for slaves or slave problems.

While serving the table, Sila kept her eyes cast down, as befitted a slave, and, following Sara's lead, worked silently. Meanwhile, she managed to see everything that was going on at the table.

After the meal, Sara's round black face was beaming, her white teeth showing broadly in her big smile. "Thank you, Sila. You have been a great help. When I am alone, I am running around, trying to have the food fixed and served properly."

Sila noticed again that Sara had not bought into the lie the masters taught them—that a slave with a lighter skin was better than the slave with a darker skin. Sara was not jealous. Sila tried her best not to give offense in any way, either to Sara or to *Mefrou*.

Sila said, "I am happy too. Not one time did Master Pe pay attention to me. He didn't look up or talk to me other than one murmured 'thank you.'"

Relieved, Sara and Sila efficiently cleaned up after the family. Next, Sara took Sila to the upper floor. It was time to meet Master Pe's mother, *Mefrou* Jana.

"Remember to treat *Mefrou* Jana with the utmost care. She has a lot of pain. Her fingers are painful. She stays in her room most of the time now."

"Sara, if *Mefrou* Jana suffers from pain in the bones and fingers, Mai Yeye could make a medicine for her. We always make that medicine because Mamawa suffers from the same." Sila was eager to be of help.

But Sara was shocked. "Sila, there is no way you can treat *Mefrou* Jana with the same medication that you treat a slave. You are to use the medication Le Docteur brings for us from Punda. He is the one that decides which medicine works best, and he tells us how to use it. Make sure you ask *Mefrou* Jana first before you give her something."

Sila nodded.

"Remember to change *Mefrou* Jana's bed daily." Sara continued her explanation as she showed her the closet. "She has accidents in the night. The sheets need to be dry and fresh because during the day *Mefrou* goes back to bed. I will show you where you can wash the soiled sheets every day. The last nurse skipped this regularly, and the Master will not stand for that." Sara's voice was firm.

"Don't worry, Sara; I will do exactly as you tell me. Can you bring me to *Mefrou* Jana now?"

Sara nodded and, holding her finger in front of her lips, she slowly and noiselessly opened the door to *Mefrou* Jana's bedroom. They took some stealthy steps inside and saw that *Mefrou* was still asleep. The room was dark and reeked of a strong smell. Sara left the room taking steps backward, and Sila followed her as quickly as possible.

"What a horrible stench was that, Sara. It smelled like old urine and rotten garlic. What is it?"

Sara held her finger in front of her lips again. "Shhh, don't speak; don't wake her up. She will be angry if we do."

"Why is she so neglected?" Sila asked.

"She is not neglected. I take care of her every day. But in the night she gets up and shoves her furniture around in her room. Sometimes she walks in the house until four o'clock in the morning. She is so stocky and with her white nightgown on, she looks like a scary ghost."

Sara shuddered. "And the urine smell penetrates everything. I cannot get the smell out. She doesn't let me open the windows. She believes that bad spirits will come in her room if her windows are open. That is why she has the garlic hanging up. She believes that garlic keeps bad spirits away." Sara threw her hands in the air. "There is just nothing I can do for her. She is the *Mefrou*. If she wants to live in a room full of rotting garlic, I need to take care of her in that smelly room. It was Le Docteur that suggested the garlic in the first place." Sara shook her head. It was too much for her to understand.

Sila pinched her nose. "That garlic doesn't keep only the bad spirits away. It would keep anybody away." The odor still lingered in her nostrils.

"*Mefrou* Jo never goes up to *Mefrou* Jana's room, and Master Pe goes early in the morning and stays at the door. He tried to change things. His mother gets hysteric when he opens the windows. I am the only one that works in that room like that."

"What time am I supposed to take care of her? Should I wake her up?" Sila asked.

"Sometimes she throws things or calls for the Master if I wake her up. We just wait till she calls us. She will be waking up soon. Let's help a little in the kitchen with the preparation for the lunch, and as soon as we hear her, we will come upstairs again."

Indeed, it didn't take long. Just when Sara and Sila finished preparing the dining room table for lunch, they heard the bell summoning them upstairs.

Mefrou Jana was awake.

They took the stairs two steps at a time.

"Good morning, *Mefrou*," Sara said with her eyes cast down.

Mefrou didn't pay attention to her. "Who is this?" she barked. "I don't want strangers in my room. OUT!"

"*Mefrou*, this is not a stranger. It is your new slave girl. She is going to take care of you. Didn't Master Pe speak with you before he left this morning?" Sara hurried to give this explanation since *Mefrou* Jana already took a step towards them. "Master Pe bought her from Master Jan in Punda for you. She arrived yesterday." Sara kept her eyes down while she spoke. Her tone was soft and mellow.

"My new slave?" *Mefrou* Jana stopped in her track and mulled over this development. Then she barked to Sila, "Nikker, come here! I want to see you better."

Sila held her hands firmly clapped together in front of her and didn't dare look up. She shuffled a tiny step forward in the direction of that strange crackling voice.

"Good... good day, *Mefrou*." Her voice faltered. The rotting garlic smell tried to suffocate her. When she dared to take another step in the direction of

Mefrou, the urine smell became overwhelming. She gagged. Her stomach protested loudly and promised to pour its contents out.

Mefrou quickly came closer and took Sila by the arm. "Open your mouth, slave, so I can look at your teeth." She grabbed Sila by the chin, yanked her face up, and said impatiently, "Open your eyes, slave, and look up. I want to see your face!"

Sila, still held by her chin, opened her eyes and looked the *Mefrou* in the face. She never had been so close to one of her Masters before. She could clearly see *Mefrou's* face and eyes and her skin, thin like parchment and almost colorless. Sila could see the blue veins running under her pale skin. Her lips were also thin, colorless, and pressed together in a nearly straight line. Her eyes were gold speckled.

"Open your mouth," said the *Mefrou* at that moment. "I want to see your teeth. Now."

Sila, afraid, clapped her mouth shut instead of opening it.

"Slave, I told you to open your mouth."

Sila looked over at Sara for support, but Sara stood as still as a statue, pondering the ceiling, and did not appear to notice anything weird going on.

Sila was alone.

Slowly, Sila obeyed, opening her mouth for the eccentric *Mefrou* to take a look.

Chapter Eight

Mefrou inspected the teeth with care, checking first the upper palate before moving on to the lower palate.

"Good teeth," she declared, and rubbing her hands, she laughed a satisfied laugh. "Good teeth make good slaves. That is what my father used to tell me when he went to Zuurzak to buy our slaves. I went with him many times and I know how to buy a good slave. My father would even buy a sick or dirty slave if he had good teeth. Our Fito would make sure they got cleaned up and healthy enough to work. As soon as they could walk my father would put them to work to make his money back. Yes, good teeth are important."

Mefrou kept watching Sila as she spoke.

"You are too white to come from a boat."

With keen eyes she kept inspecting Sila and pulled the hair wrap loose. She looked at the hair and then screamed to Sara:

"Where have you gotten this white child?"

"She is a mulatto slave, *Mefrou*. She was not born in Africa. Her parents are Criollo."

"Her mother might be a Criollo but her father is more than a Criollo for this child to be so white. Ha ha ha."

Mefrou liked her own joke and laughed with glee.

"My guess is that a master erred in finding his sleeping room and went to the wrong door one night," she cackled.

Both her slaves stood still with their eyes cast down and in the proper slave position.

Suddenly *Mefrou* stopped laughing and said with a composed voice,

"Sara, leave us, I think I might like this nikker that you brought me. She is not as ugly as the others you brought."

Sara didn't need more prompting. With two backward steps, she went through the door and left.

Sila sensed more than saw the relief Sara felt at that moment. She wished she could be the one that was allowed to leave the sickening stench. She looked wishfully at the closed window. Before she knew it, she took some tentative steps toward one of the windows. She kept her proper body posture and her eyes cast down while she asked:

"Would you like me to open the windows for you, *Mefrou*?"

She didn't wait for the answer but threw the window as quickly as possible open. The fresh clean air was like a balm for her. She gulped a big clean breath, knowing full well it might be her last.

Mefrou Jana was paralyzed for a second. Then she ran as rapidly as her old legs could carry her to the window, screaming:

"Close it, close it!"

She pushed Sila to the side and tried frantically to close the heavy wooden window. It was difficult for her because Sila stood with her arms wide spread in front of the window, trying to get as much fresh air as possible before she obeyed her mistress.

"*Mefrou*," she said in a rush, "my mother is a medicine woman. And I see that you have a lot of garlic hanging in your room. Is it not to run the bad spirits off? If you don't open the windows how do you think the bad spirits can leave?"

It took some excruciating seconds before Sila's words sank into *Mefrou*'s understanding. She stopped pulling at the heavy windows and looked at

Sila.

"Le Docteur didn't tell me that," she said. "How is it possible?"

"My mother is Mai Yeye. Have you never heard of her, *Mefrou*? She worked a lot at Zuurzak helping take care of the sick slaves and giving them medicine. Even in the time of the Tula Rebellion she was sent from plantation to plantation to heal people. She makes all her medicine herself and she taught me some. That is why I know that the windows need to be open."

Mefrou took her time thinking about this new line of medicine. Sila didn't dare say anything more. She hastened to the bed and started stripping the wet sheets. As quickly as she could she stripped the bed and put the soiled sheets in the hallway. She pulled the mattress in front of the open window so the sun could dry it a little. She made a mental note to ask Mai Yeye to sew something to cover the mattress with to prevent it soaking so much. Meanwhile *Mefrou* was still standing at the open window probably trying to take in all this new information.

Silently Sila gave thanks to Sara for telling her about the garlic. She hoped *Mefrou* didn't realize her fib. Sila doubted if she could have stayed a minute longer in that room with the galling reek of rotting garlic. Even with the windows open it was an unbearable stretch.

Mefrou didn't move from the open window. Was it possible that she liked the fresh air too? Sila didn't want to inquire and provoke her ire. She kept her head down and worked.

"Would you like me to prepare you a bath?" Sila asked politely.

"Make me a bucket with warm water. That will have to do it for today," answered *Mefrou* absent-mindedly.

"Oh, *Mefrou*, I can make you a whole bathtub. I already have water boiling over the stove. It will not take long."

Sila hoped her words did not give offence but *Mefrou* needed a bath... urgently.

"A bucket will have to do. Since I became sick I cannot bathe myself every day. My fingers are too stiff, swollen and painful. Sometimes I cannot get out of bed. I had a good slave girl, but she became sick and died on me," *Mefrou* cackled, satisfied that she outlived her much younger slave.

"I am tough to break. I will not die easily. Sara kept sending me bad slaves to take care of me. I just ran them out of my room." She rubbed her hands together and snickered.

"*Mefrou*, I know a lot about your sickness and I can help you. So you do not need to run me off," Sila said.

"Anyone is better than that blockhead Sara. She should be cleaning and washing dishes and not helping a patient like me. And that is exactly what I told my son Pe."

"*Mefrou*, I will help you. I can make you a nice warm bath and you will feel less pain after that. I will bring the dirty laundry downstairs and come back up with the hot water. Is that okay?" Sila said.

Mefrou didn't answer, so Sila took it as a yes and hurried downstairs to the kitchen to enlist her mother's help.

Mai Yeye filled a big bucket with hot water and carried it upstairs while Sila ran for cold water from the well. Upstairs again she found Mai Yeye waiting for her with the hot water outside the door of *Mefrou*'s room. Mai Yeye also had some clean sheets ready for Sila, and she had a rather large pouch with herbs with her.

"Mai Yeye, what do you have that we can put into the water to make *Mefrou* feel better?" Sila was eager to help her *Mefrou*.

"I brought some welensali leaves for you. They smell good and calm the person. They help take away pain in the bones if you use it with hot water. Just put them right in the water and let *Mefrou* sit in the tub with them. Here is some Eucalyptus too, smells good. Try them."

Sila worked swiftly. She brought the bathtub into the room, placed it behind a curtain for some privacy, filled it and added the leaves.

"You will feel much better after this bath, *Mefrou*," she promised goodheartedly.

Mefrou observed with keen eyes how Sila worked to prepare her tub. In the meanwhile she kept coming up with arguments why she shouldn't just wash herself instead of a bath. But Sila talked softly and convincing. With some coaching from her, *Mefrou* managed to ease herself into the tub. Right away she sniffed the freshness of the herbs.

"Hmm, this is good," she said.

Sila took a piece of honey soap, handmade by Mamawa, and started scrubbing *Mefrou*'s back. *Mefrou* visibly relaxed and leaned back. When the water cooled down a little, Sila refilled it with the rest of the hot water.

Mefrou soaked a long time in the bath.

Sila gave thanks for all the times she had accompanied Mai Yeye to care for the sick slaves. Those experiences came in handy today.

While *Mefrou* was in the bathtub, Sila straightened up the rest of the room. Then she carefully helped *Mefrou* dry off. She saw up close how red and swollen *Mefrou*'s fingers were. Sila knew they would be painful. With extra care she dried them off, one at the time.

Mefrou sat down and Sila combed her hair with the utmost precision, making long braids and arranging them as she saw Sara had done for *Mefrou* Jo. Sila pushed the comfortable chair between the two windows so *Mefrou* would have the most air possible.

Mefrou declined the breakfast Sila offered her but accepted a cup of tea.

Sila hurried to the kitchen to make it. Mai Yeye had already taken care of that. The tea smelled of welensali (wild sage), anise, mint, and some other herbs that Sila could not place right away. Mai Yeye explained that she put some black bark in it to take away the pain and some Valerian that should have a calming effect on *Mefrou*. Sila carried the tea with medicinal ingredients up the stairs.

Mefrou Jana sniffed the tea before asking:

"What is in this tea? It smells different."

"It is an herb combination that my mother makes." Sila hoped *Mefrou* would drink it without asking too much questions.

Mefrou looked at her cup and decided:

"It isn't too bad, I will drink it."

Sila smiled.

"Yes, *Mefrou*, you will feel better. Are you sure you don't want me to make you a sandwich? Or cook some porridge? We have fresh oats and we have fresh tamarind from the tamarind tree in the yard. I can cook it fast for you."

Mefrou Jana fixed her eyes on Sila.

"It is a long time since I had such an eager slave to serve me. Why are you like this?"

Sila stood in front of her, eyes cast down and did not answer at first. But after some time she said:

"My mother taught me to be a good worker, so *Mefrou* can be satisfied with me."

Suddenly *Mefrou* started laughing again. It sounded like a chicken running for its life.

Sila's eyes flew open. She was scared to death. Had she given offense in any way? But *Mefrou* stopped laughing and said in a normal voice:

"I never eat in the morning. I prefer to wait until lunchtime. If my hands were better I would have loved to go eat in the dining room today. It would have been a good day since I took a bath and my hair is done. It has been more than two weeks since I went downstairs."

Her voice was dejected and wishful.

"I will ask Mai Yeye if she has some of the ointment that we make for Mamawa. I think it will help *Mefrou* too. It takes away the pain and the swelling," she offered.

Mefrou Jana looked into the willing face of Sila and said doubtfully:

"Okay, go get it. But bring me the drops Le Docteur sent for me too. I need to take those every morning. Not that they help me, but I will take them anyway."

Sila hastened to the kitchen, looking for Sara to help her locate the right drops for *Mefrou* Jana.

Sara was talkative.

"How was it with *Mefrou* Jana? Did she scream a lot at you after I left?"

"No Sara, she didn't. I managed to get the windows open, and then I helped her to take a bath. She is drinking her tea and waiting for me. Where do I find her medicine?"

Sara's mouth dropped open.

"You did what? How is that possible? Usually Master Pe has to convince her to let me give her a bath. She resists baths. How did you do it?"

"Sara, please, help me, I cannot dally. I need to go back to her with her medicine."

And turning to Mai Yeye, Sila asked:

"Mai Yeye, do you have some of the ointment that you make for Mamawa? I want to use it on *Mefrou* and see if it works."

"Well, Sila," Mai Yeye laughed, "it looks like God has had mercy on you again."

"Mai Yeye sees God in everything," Sila thought, but she didn't let on.

"Here you go, Sila; I have half a calabash with that ointment. I will give you some and keep some for Mamawa," Mai Yeye offered.

Sara was jumping from one foot to another.

"You cannot touch *Mefrou*'s fingers, Sila. Really, she will not permit you and she will cuss. She might even call for Master Pe, and that on your first day of work. Please let her be, Sila. White people only use white people's medicine."

"I want to try, Sara. She has so much pain. I really think this might help her. I asked her permission and she gave it to me."

Turning to Mai Yeye, Sila implored:

"Pray that she doesn't scream for the Master."

Back in the room Sila found *Mefrou* asleep in her comfortable chair. Sila looked down on her wrinkled face.

"This old lady who cannot even wash herself owns me. She has the power to punish me until death with no questions asked. I am her property. I belong to her for always."

A big sigh escaped Sila as she contemplated her position in life.

"At least I will not have to serve the Master in the night and make babies for him to sell." She tried to cheer herself up.

Sila decided to let her *Mefrou* sleep. It was probably the hot bath and the medicine working. In the meantime she cleaned up the tub, turned the mattress and made the bed. She swept the room. On the table she put some water in a big bowl and broke small green mint leaves in the water. Immediately the room started smelling better.

She stood still in front of the garlic hanging from the walls and the doorposts. Should she be so bold and take them down? She didn't dare to do it. Maybe in a couple of days.

"Slave, are you back?" Sila heard the voice of her *Mefrou* and she whirled around.

"*Mefrou*, I brought your drops with me, here they are."

Mefrou Jana opened her mouth and indicated Sila to give her the drops. Her eyes were pinched closed.

"Huh," she shuddered. "Bad stuff, so bitter, if it only worked...." she complained.

"My mother sent some of her ointment for you, *Mefrou*. It has brandy in it. It will help you against the pain I think. Would you please try it?"

Hopeful, Sila held the calabash out to show her *Mefrou* the ointment.

"Maybe tomorrow, Sila," *Mefrou* said. "My hands are too sore today to put ointment on them. I cannot even open them."

"*Mefrou*, I can help you. I can apply it for you on your knuckles and when the pain subdues a little, I can apply it in your palms for you."

Mefrou looked doubtfully at the crude calabash covered with a piece of flour sack. She finally relented.

"Make sure I do not feel any pain, or..."

Sila took the calabash and scooped a little ointment out of it. Slowly, very slowly, she applied the thick, fatty white paste to the red and swollen knuckles. Little by little she massaged it into the fingers. Turning *Mefrou*'s hands, she applied it to the palms.

Mefrou Jana was quiet and sat back in her chair with no sign of being in pain. Sila breathed again.

Mefrou drifted into a relaxed sleep. Sila tip-toed out of her room.

Chapter Nine

It was almost lunchtime, and Sila helped Sara bring the hot food into the dining room where the family would be eating. Master Pe walked in, red from the sun and dusty from the plantation work. Sila hastened to hold a big calabash filled with clean water for him to wash his hands and face.

He nodded his thanks.

Mefrou Jo came in with their daughter, Yufrou Wilhelmina. As always, the ladies didn't bother to acknowledge the slaves. They sat down, and *Mefrou* nodded to Sara to serve the meal.

The dining room door opened once more, and *Mefrou* Jana walked in, fully dressed.

Master Pe jumped up. "Mamai, how are you? I didn't know you would be coming down today. When I came into your room early in the morning you was still sleeping."

"Sara, put another plate on for *Mefrou* Jana," *Mefrou* Jo ordered, but Sara already had the plate in place.

Sila stood next to the door, observing from under her eyelashes. When *Mefrou* Jana took her knife and fork with her own hands, her family was in for another surprise.

"Mamai! You can use your hands today?" Master Pe stood up from his place and walked over to his mother to examine this.

"I know," said *Mefrou* Jana with a smile. "It is the medicine the slave girl brought for me."

"Who brought what medicine for you, Mamai?" Master Pe didn't understand.

"I don't know her name, but Sara brought her for me. Her mother is a medicine woman who worked on Zuurzak. You know Zuurzak where Pa always bought his nikkers?"

"But Mamai..."

Mefrou Jana cut him off. "I want to eat now, son. With food in my stomach I can answer many more questions." *Mefrou* Jana filled her plate with rice, chicken, peas, and corn.

Master Pe and *Mefrou* Jo looked each other in the eyes, and Master Pe shrugged.

"Sara," Master Pe inquired, "what is my mother talking about?"

"It is *Mefrou* Jana's new slave girl, Master. Her name is Sila; here she is." Sara shook visibly, and thick sweat drops appeared on her face. Quickly she pushed Sila to the front. "Her mother is a medicine woman, and they had an ointment especially for this kind of ailment, Master. She used this ointment, and she helped *Mefrou* Jana in a bathtub."

"Mamai, did you take a bath today?" Master Pe was, if possible, more confused.

"Can I eat my food in peace now? You all can discuss my ailments and personal hygiene after my meal." *Mefrou* Jana's tone was definitive. "I need to hurry up with these fingers; I don't know how long they will stay open, and I wish to do some more things before they are all painful and swollen again."

Her matter-of-fact statement broke the ice, and the family laughed. Even Sila gulped a couple of times to keep a straight face.

Right after lunch, Master Pe brought his mother to her room to see the medicine for himself. When he opened the door, he stood still for one moment. "What is going on here? Mamai, how come you opened the windows?" He looked around and saw the clean, fresh room, the smelling bowl on the table, the clean bed, but most of all he noticed the fresh air. Now he really wanted some answers.

So did his wife, who was back in his sitting room waiting for him.

"What did Mamai say about her hands?" she inquired.

Master Pe described the room to her and all the changes he had noticed. "When Jan sent his Fito in the middle of the night to ask me if I still needed a slave girl for my mother, I knew that something was going on. But what could I do? He is powerful in the city, Punda, and I need him. So I said yes. Then he showed up with three slaves instead of one and a baby."

"Is it true that they are medicine women then?" his wife asked. "That is what Jan said, but I thought he was trying to make them sound more interesting for me. Now I realize that he might have been speaking the truth."

"That means that we have three medicine women for free? That is strange."

"I don't remember that I have paid special attention to our new slaves. I assumed the Fito and Sara would break them in and that they would do their job. It is time I speak with them myself," Master Pe announced, as he rang the bell and waited for Sara to call the women to his study.

Fearfully, the three women shuffled into the study. Once inside the room, they stood with their backs against the wall in the proper posture.

"Come in, I want to speak with you," the Master said.

Mamawa was the first one to dare to move closer to the Master. "What do I have to lose? I am old and almost dead anyway. It is by God's grace that I am still on this earth," she thought.

Quietly they awaited the word from their Master.

"Where are you from?" Master Pe demanded.

"We come from the Town House of Master Jan. Two days ago Master Jan brought us here to serve you and your family."

"I know Master Jan brought you here, but why? Why four of you? Why here?"

Mamawa was the first to answer again. "Master, we don't know. We are only slaves. Our Master told us to come, so we came. We will serve you well."

"How old are you?" Master Pe wanted to know after he observed her.

"I am very old, Master. I came to this country on a slave ship. I have seen many slaves come and go. I saw Tula fight, and I have seen many die. I have had eight sons. They are all gone now. I live with these women. They take care of me, and I take care of them. We are a family, Master. I am a powerful medicine woman, and I have taught them all my skills. I can use herbs to make medicine to heal your slaves. Master, please let us stay here together. We will be good for you. Do not sell us and separate us, please, Master."

"I am not planning to sell you," Master Pe assured them when he realized that they were frantic with worry. "I want to know who treated my mother and what you used."

Sila took a very small step towards the desk. "I helped *Mefrou* Jana, Master, my mother makes this medicine for Mamawa, and it works well for us."

"Explain to me how you make that medicine."

"This medicine can easily take half a day to prepare. Sometimes we cannot make it because we don't have all the ingredients that we need to prepare it. We cook the fat of the pork a long time, until it dissolves and becomes fluid. In this fat we put some brandy. That is the most difficult part of this medicine—to find the brandy. In this ointment we put some mint, eucalyptus, and black bark. They all help with the swelling and take the pain away for some time." Sila rattled off all the ingredients.

Now that the talk turned to medicine, Mai Yeye felt free to join the conversation. "But the green leaves of the welensali also works good for some people, Master. We just need to try and see which one works better for *Mefrou* Jana. If one doesn't work, I just keep trying till I find something that does. I have noticed that rainy weather multiplies the pain, so then we use much more hot tubs or hot compresses."

"But how do you find brandy?" Master Pe wanted to know.

"In the time I worked on Zuurzak, I could get a square bottle to help cure the slaves. But since

I don't go there anymore... Sometimes we ask our Master for a small glass of brandy, and he would grant it," Mai Yeye explained.

Master Pe kept firing questions at his slaves, trying to find a hole in their story, but they could answer all of them with simple statements that made sense to him.

"How much ointment do you have?" he asked at last.

"Right now we don't have so much, Master. We moved to this plantation without too much time to prepare, so we could not bring all our herbs with us. If Master permits it, I could keep a small patch of herb garden next to our room so we will have always enough herbs growing," said Mai Yeye.

"Which plants do you need?" the Master wanted to know.

"For pain in the bones or swollen fingers, I use plantain leaves. I make a cataplan out of it. If we have cotton balls, I can use them in the cataplan, and they help ease heavy pain. I do have welensali leaves but still need black bark and aloe to help me cure wounds and infections. I use a mixture of aloe and prunes to help people that need to be cleaned inside," Mai Yeye said.

Master nodded often when Mai Yeye was speaking, encouraging her to tell him more. When she finished, he announced, "You have permission to cultivate a small herb garden next to your house. Let Fito know all that you need to get started. What else do you need to make that ointment for my mother?"

"We do not have brandy, Master."

"I will let Fito buy a box of brandy. I want you to have enough of that ointment at hand. There might be other people suffering from the same affliction. If you take good care of my mother, you will have a fine life on my plantation," promised Master Pe, and his wife nodded.

****

As soon as the women left the room, *Mefrou* Jo went to her husband and exclaimed, "Pe, I think we just won the lottery!"

****

In the kitchen Sila said, "What can this be? Why would Master Pe treat us so politely?" Sila looked at her mother for an answer, but she didn't know either. Mamawa came up with the only logical explanation that she could provide. "I believe God just gave us grace in the eyes of our Master." She hugged her child and grandchild and almost squeezed Didi by doing so. They all laughed and cried together, and for this one time Sila almost believed.

****

In the room upstairs, the Master said to his wife, "They were frantic, thinking that I was planning to sell them. I didn't tell them that I couldn't sell them. Not even if I wanted to—because they are not mine. Jan didn't sell them to me. I just promised Jan to keep them here for him until he comes back for them."

Chapter Ten

Back to 1827 ...

It didn't matter how good the masters were to Sila, she never recovered enough from her traumatic experience with Master Jan to trust anyone. That is why she hid Didi from her Master's eyes as long as possible. She didn't want history to be repeated with her child.

She kept her sweet child, who had been a blessing over the years, busy with collecting the medicinal herbs, washing, cooking in the kitchen—anything, just to keep her out of sight. It worked for 12 years.

Now it looked as though it had come to an end. *Mefrou* had just waited long enough for Didi to be well prepared for her daily tasks. How was it possible that just when Didi knew how to take care of house jobs, *Mefrou* could think...and speak those horrible words?

"I'm sure we'll find a good place for her."

A good place...a good place...

Sila's thoughts were jumbled in her head. Haven't I suffered enough? Haven't I always served with my heart and soul? Shouldn't I get to keep my own daughter? She could not understand how she could stand in front of *Mefrou* and listen to those horrible words. How could *Mefrou* be so...so...selfish?

Almost on "automatic pilot," Sila finished her morning duties and served the table at the noon meal. It amazed her that she was able to finish serving the meal without a major catastrophe. Afterward she brought the dirty dishes to the kitchen where Didi was waiting to wash them.

When she saw her mother's face, Didi asked her, "Mai, what happened?"

Sila couldn't talk with her daughter at that moment. She said, "Didi, do the dishes and clean the kitchen for me, can you? I will serve the coffee and then I will go lie down a little. I have a terrible headache."

"Mai, I will make you a cup of chamomile tea in the meantime."

Sila went to her small, dark room. She mourned—again—for her grandmother Mamawa who passed away the year before. Mamawa would have prayed right away! Mai Yeye was in the slave quarters helping a young slave girl deliver her baby following a difficult pregnancy. She would not be back soon. Sila was alone.

Sila lay on her mat, with a cloth stuffed into her mouth to muffle the sounds. Her body bent forward, over and over as she screamed silently.

"*Mefrou* wants to sell my baby...*Mefrou* wants to sell my baby..."

She wished she could pray. She struggled to understand faith in God and the fact that she was still a slave. How could she trust God? Nothing had changed in all those years. Didi was a young woman now and remained a slave. And all of God's promises were written in that German Bible. She could not understand how Mai Yeye's faith could grow so strong.

Now they had prayer meetings on the plantation. The slaves gathered early Sunday morning before daylight under the guidance of Papa Bubu. Sila had been in the meetings many times but still she was uncomfortable. How can a slave speak about freedom in God?

Every week Papa Bubu would show them "the book." One of his old masters gave that book to him and he guarded it with his life. "It is the word of God," he said week after week.

Sila felt like going to Papa Bubu. But the work in the Big House waited. *Mefrou* might ring for something else and she still needed to clear the coffee table.

Sila forced herself to take control, and because of a lifetime of keeping all the slavery rules, she managed to do so.

In the middle of the night, Mai Yeye came back to their room. A crying Sila clung to her mother and explained what had happened. Quietly they sat there in the dark.

"Did *Mefrou* tell you she was going to sell Didi?"

"Yes, she said she was going to find a good place for her."

Mai Yeye looked over at her grandchild, who was sleeping peacefully, and said, "Let's pray, Sila. Let's pray for help. Remember how God saved us from Master Jan and *Mefrou* Victoria when Didi was a baby? Why would He save Didi then and let this new master sell her? God will help us. Let us believe."

"Mai Yeye, I already tried to pray but I am not sure God heard me." Sila looked down and wiped a tear from her face. "I...I...might have been...a...little angry with God," Sila confessed, trembling. "How come we are still slaves?"

Mai Yeye prepared herself for prayer and responded, "I know, Sila. I know it is difficult. God knows too. How much longer will we be slaves? Let us pray together and let us get some sleep. God will make a way out again. As He always does. And when He does, this time I want you to promise God that you will never doubt Him again."

Sila nodded slowly while she observed Mai Yeye, who now looked old. Her feet were swollen, proof to Sila of how tired she was. Sila was proud of her mother. She was a strong slave. Her faith permitted her to be a beacon of rest for Sila, Didi, and many more. It was almost like slavery could not hold Mai Yeye.

Their life had changed drastically in these past 12 years. First *Mefrou* Jana died peacefully in her sleep, without pain. Then Mamawa passed away in the same calm manner. Sara became too old for the heavy work in the house. She was content making alpargatas, the traditional handmade sandals made with cotton and jute rope. Sila took over all the housework.

In the years that the medicine women served the Masters, a mutual respect had developed between them. *Mefrou* Jo depended completely on Mai Yeye for her household. And she trusted each woman entirely.

It was an even bigger change when *Mefrou* Jo and Master Pe moved to the Netherlands to live with their family there for some years. Yùfrou Wilhelmina, their daughter, married Master Moron and she became the new *Mefrou* of the house.

They were good masters but not like *Mefrou* Jo and Master Pe. *Mefrou* Wilhelmina and Master Moron could ignore the slaves. Slaves were there to serve them and not to bother them.

****

If it were not for her concerns about Didi, Sila would have been a happy worker, rising at five in the morning in order to get the work done. *Mefrou* Wilhelmina was easy to get along with when you served her well. She never took the belt or the whip to the women. Of course, she had had a good example in her mother, *Mefrou* Jo.

Sila made sure her *Mefrou* didn't need to ask for things. She was always a step ahead, ready with what her *Mefrou* wanted next, just like her mother and grandmother taught her.

****

The next day, Sila got up early as usual and fetched water for the Big House and for the kitchen. When Mai Yeye joined her in the kitchen, they prayed. They enlisted the help of Papa Bubu and the prayer group. For weeks everybody was calling upon God for Didi's well-being.

Mai Yeye's faith remained strong that God would make a way out for Didi. Mai Yeye kept repeating that God would "come up with something," and she refused to despair or to let Sila despair.

Following *Mefrou*'s order, Sila let Didi assist at the table. Sila could see *Mefrou* Wilhelmina casting her eyes on Didi. The more she realized *Mefrou*'s interest in Didi, the harder Sila prayed.

In that week, Papa Bubu was sent to work on Plantation Roi Santu. He was a renowned handyman. The Master used to rent him out to other plantations. Papa Bubu didn't mind being rented out even when he didn't get any money for his hard work. He used the time to tell the other slaves on the plantations about God. He taught them, answered questions, and relayed the biblical teachings that he knew. In this way he sharpened his knowledge.

Some of the slaves in other plantations could spell, and one could even read simple things. But none knew German.

Papa Bubu's absence was hard on the prayer group during this difficult time. A big black field slave, Roy, took over and came to visit Mai Yeye daily for prayers and encouragement. He was strong in his faith and Sila leaned on him for encouragement.

Mefrou ordered Mai Yeye to teach Didi to cook—which Didi could do already—and to sew and bake. She wanted Didi to be trained as a competent housekeeper and a medicine woman. On different occasions she asked Sila how Didi's skills were progressing.

Fearfully Sila started mulling over the possibility of escaping and taking Didi with her. Escaping would not be difficult now since nobody really kept track of the women. They were free to come and go. Sometimes Sila spent a whole day in the woods collecting herbs and another day over the fire cooking them.

On those days, Mai Yeye and Didi would take charge of the household. *Mefrou* would not miss her if she didn't come into the house for a day or two. Maybe Papa Bubu could help her when he came back. He had been to so many places, he would know where slaves hid when they escaped. Sila could not share her thoughts with her mother; she tried but Mai Yeye simply refused to even think about that.

Under heavy strain, the women kept facing each day, one at a time. On a Sunday morning, Mai Yeye was called into the private sleeping room of the masters. Usually the slaves had a couple of hours free after they served Sunday brunch. But this day Mai Yeye didn't come back to their little hut.

Sila sat with Didi in the cool breeze under the big tamarind tree south of their room. Didi was trying to sew a new apron—one of the things *Mefrou* wanted her to do—and Sila was supposed to help her. But she could not concentrate. What was going on? Why was Mai Yeye in *Mefrou's* room for so long?

She sent a boy to call Roy. Roy came by with four other women and they all prayed together. When it was getting late, Sila sent Didi to the kitchen of the Big House to start preparing dinner and to keep them updated if she saw something. The prayers kept going up and the tears kept streaming.

Finally, after many hours, Mai Yeye came out of the Master's room. She ran to them when she saw them sitting in a huddle under the tamarind tree.

"Sila, all is well. God has done it again! Praise God! We get to keep Didi!"

She threw her arms around Sila and they both laughed and cried at the same time.

"Mai Yeye, how did it happen? Are you sure?"

"*Mefrou* is expecting a baby and her pregnancy is not an easy one. Le Docteur had instructed the Master to buy a healthy young slave girl to serve *Mefrou* solely and to take care of the baby when it is born. It is unlikely that *Mefrou* will be able to care for the baby." Mai Yeye was out of breath from running but she plunged ahead.

"That is when I said to the Master, 'We don't need to buy another healthy young girl. We have Didi and we have trained her as a medicine woman. She will be able to help *Mefrou* and I will assist her. We can do it, the three of us.' And he agreed."

"He agreed?"

"Yes, he agreed."

"He agreed!"

All the women and Roy kept repeating the same words while they laughed and praised the Lord.

It was much later when Roy brought them all back to the present. "How sick is *Mefrou*?"

With that simple question, he managed to bring into focus a whole new and bigger problem: a sick master. There was not one slave that wanted a sick master. Life was hard enough with healthy masters and could only become harder with sick masters. The stress of sickness was enough to provoke many masters into resorting to whippings that they would not have done otherwise. Worse than that was the uncertainty of their faith.

The prayer group decided then and there to pray for *Mefrou* and the baby. And there was no time like the present to begin.

Chapter Eleven

In the following days, *Mefrou* was often too sick to come to the table. Le Docteur became a regular visitor. The Master gave Fito some of his daily tasks and did not go to the fields so often. All the slaves were in suspense.

Didi started her new job without delay. She spent most of her time in *Mefrou*'s room, tending to the invalid. When *Mefrou* slept, Didi stood next to her bed with a big fan and kept her cool. She helped *Mefrou* make some small baby clothes and prepared a bed for the new baby. *Mefrou* had extreme difficulty with eating and was sick until the 8th month of her pregnancy. Mai Yeye made cups of tea to try to soothe her stomach. Didi spent many hours preparing food and spoon feeding her *Mefrou*.

The prayer group kept active.

Quite unexpectedly, *Mefrou* was ready to give birth. It was too early. Concerned, Mai Yeye sent a boy to Papa Bubu to ask for prayers. She also sent for the Fito and asked for a slave girl to come help in the kitchen for the day. She took Sila with her to the sick room to help Didi.

Master Moron was pacing around in the room. His hair was disheveled and his eyes were red. Didi fanned *Mefrou* while she tossed and turned. She was weeping uncontrollably. The women quietly prepared for delivery. They brought extra blankets, boiled water, and brought several calabashes in case the doctor needed to wash his hands. They prepared different teas. The bed was placed on high stubs to raise it. They helped *Mefrou* out of her clothes and into a nightgown. In the meantime, Didi stripped the bed and put a tick mat, made of many layers of flour sacks stitched together, over the mattress to protect it and proceeded to make the bed again. Once it was ready, they helped *Mefrou* get comfortable.

Mai Yeye had the salt and wraps ready for the infant by the time Le Docteur arrived. He brought his own nurse with him, but he nodded his satisfaction when he saw that everything was in place. He was ready to start. The delivery was painful and exhausting for *Mefrou*. It took most of the day and half of the night for the small white baby boy to arrive. But there he was: baby Christian.

From that moment on, Didi became his "Yaya," or nanny, during the day and the night.

The nurse cleaned the baby and wrapped him in his blanket, refusing the salt Mai Yeye offered. She gave the too small, too quiet baby to the slaves and said, "Take him to his room and care for him while Le Docteur helps your *Mefrou*. Do you have a wet nurse?"

Didi nodded, "Yes ma'am, Fito brought a wet nurse yesterday. She is already in the baby's room. She will feed him." Didi didn't mention that Mai Yeye was strongly against that procedure. "Every baby should have milk from his own mother," Mai Yeye kept repeating. Since there wasn't a thing that the slaves could do about this practice, they obeyed and brought the baby to his wet nurse.

Mai Yeye cautioned Didi saying, "You need to be very careful now, Didi. I think the baby is too small to make it. We should not let him cry. I know how easy such a small one can slip away." A look of concern spread across Mai Yeye's face as she looked at the baby. She wanted to tell her *Mefrou* to keep the baby and nurse him herself, that a wet nurse was not a good idea for such a weak newborn. But there was no way her voice would be heard.

Didi nodded somberly. A heavy responsibility rested on her shoulders now. "Will you come help me, Mai Sila?"

"Of course, I would not leave you alone with him. Do not worry. Until we get him big, strong and healthy we will be right there with you, either Mai Yeye, the wet nurse, or me," Mai Sila reassured her daughter.

The baby was delivered to the wet nurse, and Didi stayed with them while the others went back to clean the room, tend to the Masters, and prepare a room for the nurse, who would stay after Le Docteur left for Punda. It was almost daylight when they finished.

Early in the morning, when it was still dark outside, Didi came timidly to find Mai Sila and Mai Yeye. They were still up in the kitchen trying to wash the soiled sheets in a tub of hot water.

"There is something wrong with baby Chris," Didi said, shaking visibly. "He doesn't want to drink. His wet nurse has done everything she could. Her breasts are hurting her; she needs the baby to stop crying and drink her milk. Come quick and help us."

The situation was worse than they thought. Baby Chris was red from crying. The nurse was frantic, trying over and over to get the baby to nurse, but he refused.

Mai Yeye said to Didi, "Go get the Master. He is in the library. I just brought him a cup of coffee. Tell him to come quick."

Didi ran to the library. She knocked and entered the room after the Master gave her permission. Master Moron was smoking a pipe and he didn't look up.

Didi stood still, hands clasped in front of her, face down, in the position required for a slave until the Master would give her permission to speak. After some time he looked up.

"Didi? What do you want?"

"Master, baby Chris does not want to nurse from his slave. And he is too small to cry... he cannot be crying so long... and not eating. I... I... I..."

The Master jumped into action. "Where is the baby?"

"He is in his room with his wet nurse and Mai Yeye, Master."

Master Moron was already on his feet, striding purposefully to the nursery. Turning the corner, he heard his baby crying uncontrollably. He threw the door open and burst in.

Didi followed him and saw the wet nurse slave standing in the middle of the room, sweat streaming from her wide black face, with the baby in her arms. She was softly singing lullabies for the baby, swinging him gently. Baby Chris refused to be comforted and continued to cry pitifully.

"Give him your breast, woman!" Master Moron barked. He walked to her and swiftly gave her a smack on her face. Hastily, the wet nurse, forgetting all modesty, pulled out her ample breast and offered it to the baby. A stream of milk splashed over the baby's face and over her arm. Everyone in the room could see how full her breasts were. She put the baby tenderly at her breast but he rejected it. The precious liquid streamed from him onto the floor. The baby screamed even harder. His small face was red and puckered. He was a miserable child.

Mai Yeye took a full step forward and said, "Master, this baby needs his mother. He is too small and too weak to survive on his own. If Master permits it, I will make a special tea for *Mefrou* to help her make enough milk to be able to nurse her own baby."

Master Moron's eyes shot fire, but he could clearly see that the wet nurse did what she was supposed to do. There was nothing he or anyone could do. He ordered Mai Yeye to take the baby to her *Mefrou*.

Immediately Mai Yeye took charge. Sending Didi flying for the tea, she took the baby from the wet nurse and walked to the room of their *Mefrou*, who was lying in bed as if she were in a coma. Her skin was a ghostly white and her lips almost blue.

Master Moron softly shook *Mefrou*, stirring her out of her deep slumber. He explained the situation, and although she didn't understand completely, she agreed to try to feed the baby.

Her nurse, dressed in a starched white uniform with a stiff nurse's cap on her head, stretched out her hands to take the baby from Mai Yeye. But Mai Yeye held firmly to her charge. This was her baby. She turned her back to the nurse and moved closer to her *Mefrou*. She spoke to her in a low, comforting voice while she helped her turn onto her side. She worked quickly. Then she asked Master Moron and the nurse to step back. Didi started fanning *Mefrou*.

Sila expertly cleaned the breast of *Mefrou* with a wet cotton ball. Mai Yeye positioned baby Chris on the breast. Amazingly, they saw how he lurched for the nipple and started gulping hungrily. Immediately the room was quiet with a serene quietness.

Mai Yeye used some wet cotton to wipe *Mefrou*'s forehead. Her mind went through her medicine pouches, wondering what she could make to help *Mefrou* regain her strength. Didi handed the fan to Sila and hurried to the kitchen.

Master Moron and the nurse slowly came closer. They observed the serene scene in the room.

"My medicine women are very knowledgeable," Moron whispered to the nurse, as though in awe at what he had just witnessed.

"Yes they are," the nurse agreed. "How did you acquire such capable women? Did you train them?" she asked.

Master Moron shrugged, "I don't know; I certainly did not train them and I have not seen much of them since I moved here. They are always so quiet and they stay in the background. I have not paid too much attention to them. They seem to bring me just what I want before I ask for it. That is probably why I never noticed them too much."

"You certainly notice them now!" his nurse said. "If they had not brought that baby back to its mother, he could have died. He is a small one, but if he keeps drinking like he is doing now, he will survive," she reassured him. "It is time now for me to take over the care of your wife. I am the nurse. Le Docteur has instructed me to do it. I cannot be sitting here watching them work. Your wife is my patient."

But Moron laid his hand on hers and held her

back when she was ready to go claim her position.

"You just sit here and let them do it. They are doing a good job."

The nurse bit her lip.

Didi knocked and came in with a plate of food and hot tea for *Mefrou*.

****

Didi had used the black bark that Mai Yeye had left ready on the table. The medicine women always used this to clean the womb of a postpartum patient. Didi used some of the crushed sesame seeds mixed with honey to make a batch of tasty cookies. Sesame seeds help the production of milk. She brought all these things to the room.

She wanted to take over the fanning from Mai Sila, whose hands would be heavy after so much fanning, but Mai Sila sent Didi on another errand first.

"Didi, go get the cushy big chair from the library and bring in here to *Mefrou*'s room. I want a big chair ready for when *Mefrou* wants to sit up."

Didi came back with the chair, and Mai Yeye helped her situate it in just the right spot. Then Didi raced off to fetch a small table, which they put next to the chair.

Master Moron sat quietly in the corner and observed the women as they worked. Mai Yeye walked respectfully to him and stood still with her head inclined, waiting for permission to speak. When he gave her permission with a small nod, she said simply, "Master, the baby is too small to survive on his own, he will need special care."

Master Moron's face turned white, and his eyes shot open. "I have sent Fito already to Punda to bring Le Docteur back," he said, tumbling over his own words.

Mai Yeye nodded quietly and asked permission to speak again. "I think we should try to keep the baby close to *Mefrou*'s heart for a long period of time, Master," she said. "He needs her body warmth to stay on temperature. He needs to be close to the source of his milk so he doesn't need to cry for his food. We want to save all his energy for growing. Master, I think this will be the best chance to save Baby Chris."

Moron wiped his brows and gulped. He opened his mouth and closed it several times before he gave her permission to try what she had suggested.

Mai Yeye shook *Mefrou* Wilhelmina gently from her sleep and helped her sit up. "We have a special tea and sesame seed cookies for you, *Mefrou*," she offered respectfully.

After *Mefrou* ate and drank, Master Moron explained the plan. *Mefrou* was flustered and could not understand exactly what was going on. Master Moron called Mai Yeye closer to explain. She clarified that Baby Chris seemed to be too small and feeble to make it on his own, so that he needed to be continually cared for and kept warm.

"We can make a small pouch for Baby Chris and hang it around your neck. That way, it will be easy for you to have him with you all the time."

Mefrou Wilhelmina was too tired and confused to make a decision. She turned her head to her husband, asking for his opinion.

"Can't you send for another wet nurse, Yeye?" he wanted to know. "Maybe this woman's milk was sour."

But Yeye shook her head. "It was not sour, Master, because her own child was drinking it all the time. On the plantation all the other nursing slaves have been nursing for some time. Their milk is not good enough for a newborn baby. We would need to buy a wet nurse on the market. In two more hours Baby Chris would want to eat again. Does my lord want to trust this baby to a new slave?" Yeye tried to keep her voice as humble as possible while she waited for her words to settle in her Master's mind.

"No, we need to keep this child with us," he said. "If something happens to him my wife would die. She has been looking forward to him. And he is our firstborn. Isn't there another way to feed him so my wife can have some rest? Can't we use bottles with goat's milk?"

"I believe," she replied adamantly, "that Baby Chris needs his mother's milk to be healthy." Mai Yeye was unyielding.

The Master relented. "I think we need to try

their solution, Wilhelmina," he said to his wife.

At that moment Didi walked in and brought a blanket made of clean cotton material, the softest fabric she could find. It was one of the new blankets *Mefrou* had received in the mail from her mother in the Netherlands.

Before Master Moron or *Mefrou* could change their minds and send for another wet nurse, Mai Yeye signaled Didi to come closer and take Baby Chris. Didi then changed him, wrapped him and folded the fabric around him, making it easy to hang it on *Mefrou*'s neck. Mai Sila helped *Mefrou* sit up in her bed and they fastened the baby on her chest under a clean gown. Baby Chris slept through it all.

"For how long should I carry the baby like this?" *Mefrou* inquired. "It is very hot these days. I am not sure I can do it."

"I don't think it will be for too long, maybe three weeks?" Mai Yeye reassured her.

"Three weeks?!" *Mefrou* shrieked.

"I'm sorry, *Mefrou*, but that may be the time Baby Chris needs to be able to drink enough to sleep for three or four hours at the time. When he can do that we will know he eats enough and can grow good," Mai Yeye said.

Didi hastened to say, "I put your cushioned chair with the back to this window. See? If you sit with your back to the window you will be able to feel the cool breeze while your body keeps Baby Chris warm. And I will come into your room anytime you want, just to fan you. You will not feel hot at all."

"They have it all planned out, Wilhelmina. Let's do it for now and we will ask Le Docteur when he comes from Punda," Master Moron proposed.

The nurse rolled her eyes and left for her room.

In the following days, the women worked hard to adjust to the new routine. *Mefrou* needed continuous fanning and help with the baby. Master Moron did not return to work. With Baby Chris' needs and a frail *Mefrou* Wilhelmina, the workload was heavy for the women. On top of that, they served the nurse, who expected them to bring all her trays to her in her room.

Finally, Mai Yeye spoke with the Fito, who sent a young slave girl named Ruby to be trained to help with the housework. Fito also took the relieved wet nurse back to her own hut and baby. Didi stayed in her *Mefrou*'s room and at night slept on a mat in the corner so she could help her *Mefrou* when needed.

It took three days for Le Docteur to arrive at the plantation. When Moron told him all that had happened he said, "Well, well, Moron, you seem to have very capable slaves. I have heard of medicine slave-women, but they usually used more make-believe rituals and chanting. All the big plantation owners call on me to help them when their valuable slaves are seriously ill. I travel all around. It is the first time I have seen such capable slave medicine women."

When he saw the small pouch they made to carry the baby, he exclaimed, "Genius! I need one of these women, Moron. You need to sell me one. You have three and I need another nurse. A slave nurse would be fantastic!"

"I am very sorry but I need all the help I can get with my wife so frail and the baby so fragile. I cannot sell you one. Maybe later when things return to normal," said Moron.

With the help of Mai Yeye, *Mefrou* started walking around in the house and sitting on the porch so the baby would have some daylight. Didi stayed with them, caring for Baby Chris and fanning her *Mefrou*. Slowly all of them saw that Baby Chris was beginning to improve. He could tilt his head and he drank better and slept longer. The treatment was working!

Finally, *Mefrou* returned to the dining table, leaving the baby for a short time with his Yaya Didi. She was a careful nanny for the baby.

Life was almost normal now. Since the nurse left, Le Docteur did not need to come, and Master Moron was out in the fields again. But now a steady stream of visitors came to greet *Mefrou* and see the baby. Every day Didi dressed the little boy in his best clothes and presented him to the guests for a few minutes.

After that, she took little Chris back to his room and stayed with him. She sang to him, played with him, and kept him company while *Mefrou* entertained her friends, ate or slept.

Didi was completely absorbed in her work as a nanny. She was not doing housekeeping or kitchen work anymore. After three months, the baby was sturdy enough to be taken outside for longer periods of time. He was still a slender baby but he had spunk. He grew without major problems. He was intelligent and quick.

Didi would stroll with him over the plantation after the heat of the midday and enjoyed playing with him. He was a precious baby, and he was very attached to Didi.

As soon as he could eat, Mai Yeye spoiled him a little by putting only the most healthful things into his baby food, which she cooked herself.

Chapter Twelve

One afternoon Master Moron arrived home from his work and entered his house from one of the back doors. He hung up his hat and heard roaring laughter and clapping coming from the sitting room. He was not used to such noise in his home, so he walked to the room to see what all the commotion was about. He opened the door and saw his three house slaves sitting on the floor in a circle around his baby. They were laughing and cheering.

In the middle of the circle he saw his precious, almost one-year-old son standing! The boy was clearly delighting in all the attention that he was getting from his many "mothers." He was drooling profusely as he repeated over and over again, "dad a dad da ddda ddddda dada."

"Come, Baby Chris, one more step, let your Yaya see how good you can walk already," Didi was encouraging him.

Chris looked at her, smiling, repeating, "da dad daad da." Finally he took one more step, sending the women into gales of laughter and clapping. Then he saw his father. He quickly lowered himself to the floor and crawled to him.

The women jumped up, straightening their clothes and hair wraps. Master Moron just looked at them, speechless. With a quick nod to their Master, the slaves slipped out of the door and went to the kitchen. Didi waited in the corridor for a sign from the Master to take Baby Chris from him.

Instead, Moron took Baby Chris to greet his wife, who had just awakened from a nap, and described the scene that was still fresh in his mind. "They were sitting on the floor playing with the baby. They were cheering for him, encouraging him to take a step. They really love our child, Wilhelmina. What an irony that he will grow up and be their Master."

"Moron, you can't stop talking about the slaves, can you? From the day that I delivered, you seem to follow all they do."

"I just realized, Wilhelmina, how much our life depends on them. They could serve us with hatred, resenting us for being the masters, but our slaves are special. They don't need supervision. Even with you sick in bed, they serve us the best they can. They go beyond serving. They love our son."

****

Baby Chris had his second birthday party and was a happy, talkative child. Didi was his constant companion. She had to use all her senses to keep him in line because he loved to climb and run and could quickly get into all kinds of dangers. But Didi was young and eager and loved her charge. Nothing was too much for her when it came to her Baby Chris.

Didi was also growing up, becoming a slender young lady. She had even received her first invitation to "hold hands." The boy was Bois, whose father was Beto, a hammer smith slave who lived at the north side of the plantation. He made everything people would need for a home. Since Bois was his helper and made deliveries to the kitchen, he met Didi and was smitten.

Beto was not too happy with this development. He was a man with a vision, one single vision actually. He wanted his son to be a free man. So he worked to pay for his family's freedom. He said to his son, "I worked so hard, saving all our black coins for our freedom. In just a couple of years we will not be slaves anymore! Now you want to court a slave girl? I could not buy her freedom for you. She is a well-trained house slave, and a medicine woman on top of it. They are expensive. It will take you your whole life to work to buy her freedom. How are you going to do that? Master will give her soon to another man or take her for himself. She needs to produce children. She cannot be your wife."

Beto had tears in his eyes, for he saw that his son was determined and that nothing he could say would change that.

"Pa, she will be a medicine woman just like her ma and grandma," Bois countered. "She could work for her freedom too. I could sell her products to our clients when we go to Punda for the Master. She could be free."

"But if you marry a free woman your children will have your name. You could teach them to read. Think about that, Bois. Even if you manage to buy Didi after many years, she might be too old to give you children. Or she might have other children by the Master or by other slaves that the Master chooses."

"Pa, I believe in Didi. She is young and beautiful, she has good manners, she is an accomplished medicine woman, and she takes good care of her charge. She will be a good mother too. Best of all she never flirts with all the boys like the other girls do, and she never makes eyes with the Master or Fito. I hate women who think it is okay to share a hut with a man and still sleep with the Master. I want my wife for myself."

Although not convinced, Beto promised to talk with Didi's mother. Sila didn't like the plans either but promised to pray about it. Mai Yeye was consulted. Mai Yeye pointed out that Bois was a nice, clean boy who even could read and write a little, since his father could pay to get somebody to teach him. Mai Sila could see only that Bois was still a slave and lived far from the main house. Didi would need to share a very small hut with Bois and his whole family of six.

After long deliberation, the young couple got permission to "hold hands." It all happened just before Didi turned 15 years old. Sila quietly kept an eye on the romance as it developed slowly.

"Mai Yeye," Sila commented while looking out the window at the two young people walking together, "Didi could be jumping the broom shortly." Sila was expecting Beto any moment to come and ask permission for Didi to marry his son.

"I know, Sila, how are you feeling about that?" Mai Yeye asked.

"I'm happy Didi has a respectable boy like Bois, but deep in my heart I am disappointed. Is this it? Didi marrying and still being a slave? She will need to live in a small, hot hut and produce babies for the Master to sell or to work till death? It seems so unfair to me. I had such high hopes for our Didi. Why can't she just be a free medicine woman?" Sila clapped her hands in front of her face.

Mai Yeye gave her a quick hug. "I know what you feel. I know..."

Chapter Thirteen

Unexpectedly, *Mefrou* Wilhelmina summoned Mai Sila to order two guestrooms to be prepared for her aunt and cousin who would soon be visiting from overseas. They would stay for three months.

Sila and Yeye made the rooms airy and comfortable to accommodate the guests, not knowing that they were preparing to receive the devil himself into their peaceful world. Living in mutual respect with their Masters for so long made them forget how hard the lives of other less fortunate slaves could be.

The guests, *Mefrou* Louise and Master Jacob, arrived. She was a short plump lady with a negative look on her face. The edges of her mouth turned downward, emphasizing her natural frown. Her triple chins sagged, but her small eyes were very alert. She wore elaborate dresses, even though they were a little out of date. She knew what she wanted and demanded it in a high-pitched nasal voice.

Master Jacob was a tall, very slender gentleman, perfectly dressed, and a little effeminate. His face was red, probably from the heat. He and his mother wanted to be fanned constantly. Mai Yeye had to send for an extra slave girl from the huts to come to the house to help with the fanning while she and Sila prepared a feast for the special guests.

At the dinner table, the conversation revolved around the heat, the dust, and how dry everything was. Even when *Mefrou* Wilhelmina explained that the rains would be coming soon, the talk didn't change. *Mefrou* Louise kept complaining.

Mai Sila walked around the table to pour *Mefrou* Louise another cup of cold water. *Mefrou* Louise turned at the same moment, and they bumped into each other, with the water splashing over *Mefrou* Louise's ample bosom.

Master Jacob grinned, unashamed.

Sila was paralyzed. In all her years of serving the table, this had never happened before. "I'm so sorry, *Mefrou* ... sorry, *Mefrou* ... forgive me, *Mefrou* ..." she kept repeating.

Mai Yeye grabbed a towel and quickly came closer to help dry *Mefrou* Louise. But *Mefrou* Louise smacked Mai Yeye's hand away. She turned even redder, and her narrow eyes became narrower as she started scolding Sila. No excuses were accepted. She raised her hand and smacked Mai Sila in the face, right there in the middle of the dining room.

Master Jacob laughed again. It sounded a little off-key this time. "Moeder," he said, "Mother, do not make yourself so angry, she couldn't help it and it is only water. It will dry."

Mefrou Wilhelmina, eyes wide, looked to her husband, seeking help. A red-faced Master Moron stared back. Nobody said anything.

Sila kept serving at the table, but Mai Yeye served *Mefrou* Louise. The following days were mere repetition of that first event. *Mefrou* Louise even had a small whip in her handbag which she took to Sila or Mai Yeye on every occasion that she felt under-served.

Mefrou Wilhelmina, with her soft voice, tried to explain to her aunt that such treatments were not necessary or usual on this plantation. *Mefrou* Louise was not going to change her behavior. "You have spoiled your slaves. That is why they think they can get away with sloppy service. You need to have a strong hand with nikkers, Wilhelmina," she said.

She didn't care at all that Mai Yeye just came into the room to serve the tea tray. "The nikkers are here to serve us and they need to do it properly," *Mefrou* Louise continued triumphantly. To prove her case she took out her whip again and hit Mai Yeye completely unnecessarily and unexpectedly on her hands. The teapot would have fallen if Mai Yeye had not reacted quickly by holding it with both her hands. She could not prevent the hot tea from sloshing over her hands. With tears in her eyes she poured the tea.

Mefrou Wilhelmina looked down, embarrassed.

In the kitchen Didi and Sila discovered what happened to Mai Yeye when she tried to make herself a cold compress. Sila jumped to help her. The blisters were accumulating quickly. Didi was crying and wanted to help.

"Mai Sila ... can you ask *Mefrou* if Mai Yeye can watch Baby Chris for me during dinner so I can serve? Mai Yeye cannot work like this."

That is exactly what they did.

But from the first day that Didi served the table, things began to go worse than ever. Master Jacob gave Didi a soft pinch in the face while he said, "Wilhelmina, you have a beautiful young slave girl here. Why didn't you tell me?" And he grinned from ear to ear.

Sila's heart skipped a beat.

Didi felt an instant dislike for the guests of *Mefrou*. She could barely hide her fear as she served Master Jacob. Twice something fell out of her hand and both times Master Jacob laughed and pinched her. Didi kept glancing at her mother, trying to understand what was happening. Master Jacob did not take his eyes off her for the whole dinner, making Didi even more nervous.

***

"It is time for the truth," Sila told Mai Yeye in the kitchen.

With tears in their eyes, the women held hands. The dreaded moment had arrived. Didi needed to learn the truth. That night, before bed, the women sat down and talked seriously with Didi. For the first time she heard about her father, Master Jan, and how she came to be. Didi cried for hours. She always knew something was wrong with her but now she understood. How many times had she wondered about her father? Wanted to know about him? At a young age she learned not to ask questions about his identity.

"Didi, you can NEVER be around that man alone, do you hear me?" Mai Yeye was adamant. "You will need to hide as much as possible in the baby's room. Be careful, my little girl. That man is mean and he has his eyes on you. I saw his intentions today." Mai Sila was flexing her fingers on and off.

Didi held her tears back. She heard the words and managed to nod, but inside she was shaking in horror. Mai Yeye kept instructing her on how to avoid Master Jacob. From that day on, Didi was not to walk alone from the rooms to the kitchen. She would be escorted every minute of the day when she was out of the baby's room. She was to sleep in her corner on her mat in the baby's room and wait for her family to fetch her for dinner or to escort her when she needed to walk the baby in the yard. The plans sounded good. The first week went well and Didi managed to avoid Master Jacob's attention.

When Mai Yeye was preparing to go to the huts to help a young girl deliver, she repeated all her instructions to Didi. "I brought you some bread and a pitcher of water. If the delivery takes too long and if

I need to spend the night there, I will not come back for you. Do not leave this room. Eat here and sleep in your corner. We will check on you when I come back or in the morning. Sila is going with me."

When left alone, Didi played with Baby Chris, looked at pictures together in a picture book, changed and fed him. When *Mefrou* came to say goodnight to him he was already half asleep. Didi ate a piece of cold pancake and had a drink of water after *Mefrou* left, then stretched out on her mat. She should have brought her sewing basket. Slowly she drifted off.

A knock at the door made Didi jump with a racing heart. It was dark outside. The house was quiet. She had fallen asleep. Another determined knock. Who could it be? Surely not her mother; she would walk in, and so would *Mefrou*. Cold sweat formed on Didi's face. She looked at the door and did not move. Maybe the person would go away? Then Didi heard the voice of Master Jacob calling for her. This was it then, Didi thought. This was what her mother and grandmother had warned her about. With her heart pounding in her ears, she crawled to the corner of her mat and pressed her back to the wall, wanting to be invisible. She hung her face between her knees and folded her arms around her legs. Her ears were drumming, but she heard Master Jacob call out for her again as he rattled the door. Didi clapped her hands around her ears, hoping that he would go away. To her horror, she saw the door handle turn slowly.

Out of nowhere, a fiery determination entered into Didi. She would fight him. He would not get away with it. She jumped up and grabbed the biggest chair in the room. With the unexpected strength of a lioness, she pushed it to the door and tried to block the door handle. But the chair was too big and did not fit under the handle. Master Jacob knocked again. This time he sounded frustrated and Didi knew that she did not have more time. Now that the chair idea had failed, she had just two more options: flee or hide. She rushed to the windows and threw one open. She looked down from the third floor; it was too far down and she had nothing to climb on. A fall would kill her. There was no way to climb down to the ground or up to the roof. She rushed back and threw herself under the bed, just in time, because Master Jacob, tired of waiting, pushed the door open—chair and all—and came in.

Master Jacob's voice sounded confident when he said, "Didi, come out of your hiding place now. I know you are here. Don't make me look for you."

Didi tried not to breathe, not to give herself away.

"I have Baby Chris. Come out. NOW. Or I will drop him and tell your owner that you dropped him... on purpose."

"Oooohh." A sound escaped Didi.

Master Jacob laughed. "I knew you would not want me to drop your precious Baby Chris." He lowered his hands and Didi could see the dangling legs of the baby. He would soon awake and cry if Master Jacob kept shaking him like that.

Master Jacob laughed and Didi saw how he had already dropped Chris.

"NO!" Didi screamed and tried to reach the baby, but Master Jacob was quicker and caught him just before he hit the floor. With tears in her eyes, Didi climbed from under the bed. Master Jacob laughed again, wiggling the baby as if he would let him fall again. Didi screamed and reached out for the baby.

"Silly girl, why would you be so concerned for this baby? Don't you know that he is your owner? Don't you know that he will grow up and beat you? He could kill you with no questions asked. Why are you so devoted to him? You are a slave. He is the Master."

Baby Chris was squirming in Master Jacob's hands, making noises of discomfort.

"Master Jacob, can I have the baby please? I don't want him to cry. I need to take good care of him for *Mefrou*. She loves her baby."

"Stupid slave, do you think I care? Here, you can have your precious Master Chris. Put him back to sleep and come help me in my room. My bed is not fixed. NOW." He sneered mockingly.

Didi tried to get Baby Chris back to sleep but he started crying harder and harder and was not willing to be put down. Master Jacob, tired of waiting, grabbed Didi by the hair and pulled her with him, leaving a screaming baby behind.

In his room, Didi saw his made-up bed. Of course, Mai Sila would have made it up this morning. Master Jacob pushed her onto his bed and started pulling her dress up.

Didi screamed as hard as she could as her mother told her to do. "Somebody help me... Mai Sila... Mai Yeye, helppppppp!"

"Shut up!" Master Jacob slapped her hard on the face.

Didi screamed again. "Help, somebody help me!"

Master Jacob slapped her again and shook her violently. The door between his room and his mother's room burst open.

Mefrou Louise stood there and looked at the scene in front of her. Didi was so relieved that she began to cry softly, muttering, "Help me, help me."

Master Jacob loosened up a little but did not get off Didi. He kept her pinned on his bed.

Didi turned her eyes and saw through her tears the red and angry face of *Mefrou* Louise. "Please help me," she begged.

Mefrou Louise looked away from Didi. With her lips pursed, she focused on her son and said, "Jacob, whatever it is that you are doing, please do it quietly. I need to sleep. I don't want to be bothered by your games."

With that, she turned around and left the room. Not one word of acknowledgement for Didi. No attempt to rescue her. Nothing.

"If you scream one more time, I will have your mother and grandmother stripped and beaten in the morning. You know I can do it and I will. Shut up and open your legs," Master Jacob said in a low, threatening voice.

That night, with the inconsolable screams of the baby in her ears, Didi lost her youth.

When Master Jacob finished, he pushed her out of his bed. "Go to your precious baby, and shut him up."

When she dragged herself out of Master Jacob's room, she saw her mother and grandmother hurrying up the stairs, alarmed by the screams of Baby Chris. With one look at Didi's torn dress and tears, they knew what had happened. With open arms they held on to their precious little child. Nothing they could do took away the horrible pain Didi was experiencing. Mai Yeye took care of the baby and Mai Sila made a tea to soothe Didi. Nothing helped. She cried the whole night.

Master Jacob stayed for three months. Three long months. He would call Didi into his room with whatever excuse he could come up with. He kept her sometimes in his room sleeping on the floor so he could call her back to his bed in the morning. Didi became thin and sickly. Her smile was gone and she became afraid of her own shadow.

When the family finally left for the boat to Europe, they left the women in a greater grief. Didi was pregnant.

"What now, what now?" Sila could only cry, reliving her own misery with Master Jan, Didi's father. "Another master raping our child. Another white man's bastard. When will this ever end?"

Didi's pain was Sila's pain. And their pain was Mai Yeye's. She became old under it all.

"When Bois finds this out, he will not want Didi anymore." Mai Sila spoke the words that they all were thinking. Everybody knew Bois' strong position about girls sleeping with the masters. Mai Sila completely forgot that a year earlier she didn't want her daughter to be the wife of a slave. Now she would give anything to see her daughter married to a nice decent man like Bois—slave or not—instead of abused, hurt, broken and pregnant by a white man.

Chapter Fourteen

The grown-up Didi was unresponsive and quiet. She moved around like a ghost and did her work mechanically. Mai Yeye and Mai Sila did all they knew to help Didi, but she did not want to be helped. She slipped into a state of indifference, letting her hair go uncombed for days, refusing to change her aprons when they were soiled. She didn't sleep well at night. It was only when she was with Baby Chris that she could forget what happened to her. That is why she took even better care of her charge than before.

Didi did not have an easy pregnancy. Instead of filling out, she became skinnier. Her eyes were big in her hollow face. The smell of food made her run to empty the contents of her stomach. Mai Yeye took all her kitchen work for her so she would not be around food smells. Mai Yeye even fed Baby Chris for Didi.

One day *Mefrou* Wilhelmina called for Didi to change Baby Chris. Didi tried to hold her breath while working quickly, but it was to no avail. The smell was so sharp that Didi quickly put Baby Chris into his playpen and ran for the yard, where she vomited behind a tree. As quickly as possible she returned to her master's bedroom and apologized.

"Sorry, *Mefrou*, I think I ate something wrong today. My stomach is upset. I didn't want to become sick in your room."

Mefrou Wilhelmina was alarmed. "Are you okay, Didi? Is it a virus? Call your mother to take care of Chris."

"No, *Mefrou*, I am well now. It was just something I ate."

Mefrou was not convinced and sent for Sila. *Mefrou* kept a close watch on Didi. Later that day *Mefrou* called for Didi again.

"Didi, how are you feeling? Is your stomach ache gone?" she asked Didi.

"I am well, *Mefrou*." Her voice trembled a little under the piercing stares of her *Mefrou*, and she shuffled uncomfortably with her feet.

Mefrou stared silently at Didi, who stood in her most humble slave position waiting for what was coming. The wait felt long. She started trembling.

"Do you have something to tell me?" *Mefrou* asked in a low voice.

Didi flexed her fingers. She never felt so ashamed in her whole life. Her eyes filled with unshed tears and she couldn't answer her *Mefrou*. How could she tell *Mefrou* the awful things Master Jacob did to her? Would *Mefrou* believe her? A mere slave over a master?

Didi opened her mouth to speak but the words did not come. Her lips trembled and the tears escaped her eyes and dripped quietly over her face. *Mefrou* sat up straight in her bed and covered herself with her comforter. Her pale face was almost white.

"Speak up, child. What happened to you?" Completely unexpectedly and with a strength that she did not have for weeks, she reached for Didi, grabbed her hands, pulled her closer to the bed and screamed, "TALK!"

Didi fell down with a shriek. Suddenly, as if a candle was blown out in a dark room, Didi fainted at the feet of her *Mefrou*. *Mefrou* started screaming for help.

Mai Sila rushed into the room, unsure who was screaming. She saw her daughter, apparently lifeless, at the feet of *Mefrou*. She wanted to run to her to see what had happened. But her years of training and slave ancestry made her tend to her *Mefrou* first.

Master Moron's office door swept open and he ran to his wife's room. "What happened?" he demanded breathlessly. Baby Chris started a high-pitched howl at the top of his lungs. In all that confusion, no one had cared for him.

Mefrou was screaming, Baby Chris hollering, Didi was still on the floor, and neither Sila nor Master Moron knew what had happened. Master Moron walked quickly to his wife and tried to embrace her, but she flailed her arms wildly, pushing him from her.

Meanwhile, Mai Sila picked Baby Chris up, and he stopped screaming. With Chris in her arms she knelt next to Didi, who had already regained consciousness. With her eyes she was asking Didi what happened, but Didi could only look away.

With Didi on her feet again, Mai Sila went to her *Mefrou* and held her hands.

Mefrou Wilhelmina held on as if her life depended on it. "Sila, pray tell me, who is the father of your grandchild?"

"Oh... *Mefrou*...." Mai Sila couldn't answer. She knew that as a slave she could not say one bad word against a white guest in their home. Accusing a white Master of rape was punishable with the death sentence at worst, or a horrible beating at least. She tried to think quickly to come up with something but her lips kept trembling and forming unintelligible sounds.

"I want to know NOW, Sila! Tell me his name!" *Mefrou* insisted.

Didi pressed her back more into the wall, hoping to disappear from the scene.

Master Moron, still in the dark, said, "My goodness, Wilhelmina, what is this all about? Why do you make such a scene about the father of Didi's child?

It's most probably Bois. They were holding hands for some time now."

Master Moron's eyes searched Didi, and shaking his head, he said, "Sila, you didn't tell me your daughter was expecting. I think of Didi as a child still. Isn't she too young?"

Didi looked down and *Mefrou* shrieked again.

"Sila!" she said, "do I need to let you be beaten?"

Mai Sila's eyes opened in surprise and horror. She had never had a beating in her life, and she made sure to comply with all her Master's wishes as to avoid that.

"*Mefrou*, please, that would not be necessary. I know who the father is but I cannot tell you. It would not be my place to tell, *Mefrou*." Mai Sila's shaking voice continued, facing Master Moron now, "It is not Bois, my lord, he would never do such a thing. He is a good boy. He doesn't even know that Didi is expecting. We haven't told anyone yet."

Master Moron wanted to ask more questions but a knock at the door made them all look up.

Mai Yeye came in carrying a tray with a cup of tea for *Mefrou* and a glass of port for the Master. After serving this she said, "It is an herb tea to help calm you down, *Mefrou*. You don't need to be concerned. Nothing happened. The baby is from a stranger. It is not from anyone that lives in this house. You can be assured of that. I would not lie to you, *Mefrou*."

Master Moron took a big gulp of his port and shook his head. "Of course the baby is not from someone in the house, Wilhelmina. Fito is the only man living downstairs and he is an old man. Apart from him we don't have more men living in the house..." His words trailed off. His eyes shot wide open when understanding hit him. "Wilhelmina, did you—do you—think... that the baby is... is mine?"

Mefrou Wilhelmina started crying again.

Master Moron's face became red. The veins in his forehead stood out. He wiped off his face with the sleeve of his shirt. With an angry tone he demanded, "Didi, I want you to tell us right away who the father of your baby is. We both know that I have never touched you. Tell your *Mefrou* NOW!"

The thundering voice of Master Moron made Didi cringe more, and there was no way she could have answered. She was shaking and she looked like she would faint again at any second.

Mai Yeye quickly stepped up again. "My lord, the baby is not yours. We know that. You have always been good to us and you have never touched us. We are most grateful. We would like to continue serving my lord and the family. If my lord wished we could train this new baby slave into a good servant for this house if my lord permits us to keep the baby."

"Out!" Master Moron had had enough. "Everybody out. Didi, leave this room, take Chris. I will decide later what I will do with your baby, if we keep him or sell him. Now I want everybody out."

The women left the room.

Mefrou did not seem convinced of the paternity of Didi's child. The Master stayed for hours in *Mefrou*'s room. Sometimes the loud voice of Master Moron and the high-pitched wailing of *Mefrou* would pierce through the walls. Master Moron could not convince her.

She didn't leave her room that day or in the days to come. *Mefrou* Wilhelmina stayed in bed, sick. Mai Yeye brought tray after tray of her favorite food and drinks, but nothing could entice her lady. Fito was sent to Punda to fetch Le Docteur.

When he came, he ordered her to stay in bed.

The plantation house was unusually quiet and subdued. Didi remained sickly, and Mai Yeye had no herbs that could produce peace of mind.

Here's your passage polished with proper punctuation and structured into clear paragraphs, while keeping **every word unchanged**:

Master Moron didn't come to the dining room anymore. He would sit on the porch for hours at a time drinking strong port and smoking cigars. Sometimes he wouldn't even touch the food Mai Sila brought him on a tray.

After two weeks Le Docteur came back from town to confirm to them that *Mefrou* was expecting again. Mai Yeye knew that already and had by now started giving *Mefrou* her special herbs for a good and speedy pregnancy. With *Mefrou* sick in bed, Mai Yeye was kept busy in the house.

"Didi, child, you need to eat. I cannot have you being pregnant like that. Think of your baby. You need to have strength for the baby."

"Mai Yeye, you don't understand. I'm going to have a slave baby. Another possession for the Master. He could sell my child as soon as I have weaned him. Why would I want to have a baby that could be sold in slavery? And what will happen with the child if it is a light-skinned girl?" Didi shuddered.

"Never think that I don't understand, Didi. I know what you feel. I know how badly you want to be free. I felt the same when I was your age. Sit here and let me tell you about something that happened a long time ago."

Mai Yeye tapped on the spot next to her on the kitchen bench and served Didi a cup of herb.

"It happened when Sila was a young child. Not more than four years old I think. On the plantation where we lived at that time it was buzzing with rumors of freedom for the slaves. France had set all their slaves free on the island of St. Martin. If it happened in St. Martin it could happen here too, we were told. I prayed and prayed. I wanted to be free so badly. I knew what I would do with my freedom. I would take my child and run and never come back to wash one plate.

I was so young, full of spite for my *Mefrou* who didn't care about us but let the Master mistreat us. If it were up to me, she could wash her own dishes.

I knew how to make things. Mamawa had shown me. I could make plates, cups and buckets, using the hard calabash shell. I collected a lot of calabashes and planned to take them with me when we were free so I could sell them to people in need. I planned to be a medicine woman in Punda for all the free slaves who needed help. Oh, Didi, I had so many plans. And it was such a sad, sad, sad day when the King of France married a wicked lady who insisted that all the free black people on St. Martin would be slaves again.

We wept for weeks. I washed all the dishes I had let pile up. We were hopeless in that time. Nobody was caring for the slaves. We didn't have a strong prayer group. Until Tula. Yes, girl, you have heard about Tula. The Masters love to make fun of him. But he was a hero for us. He was a big black slave. He gave us hope. He was our champion. Through horns, tambu songs and free black men traveling in the night, we heard about him long before we saw him. Because of him, we endured slavery, knowing that he was working to set us free.

He formed a band of strong slaves who had enough; they were willing to fight for our freedom. We approved of that. We helped where we could. We sent our sons to fight with Tula."

"Mai Yeye, I never knew that!" Didi said with big eyes. "Did you fight too?"

"No, Didi, the women didn't fight with spears. We stayed behind on the plantation and in the nights we would sneak out and meet under the big trees in the far end of the property. If possible, we would try to bring water and food for our sons in hiding. We would pass along any small piece of news to the rest. Many more men were ready to take up arms at any given moment. They had enough of being slaves. They wanted their freedom and would fight and die for that right! Nothing could hold us back."

"Did you see the fighting, Mai Yeye?"

"I have not seen the actual fighting, but afterwards people told me the details. Many of our men, sons and dear ones were lost in that fight," Mai Yeye continued her story. "At first it was all good news. The slaves won the first fight at Rif St. Marie. Slave horns could be heard the whole night long. Victory hung in the air. We had such high hopes. I planned to send Sila to a school so she could learn to read and write. I couldn't sleep that night. We were so hopeful."

Mai Yeye wiped the tears from her face.

With wide eyes Didi followed the narrative. "Tell me, Mai Yeye, what happened? Why are we still slaves if Tula fought for us and won?"

"That was the first fight, my child; he won the first fight but not the second. They tricked him. They took him captive and they killed him. Not only that, but they hanged him from a tree in Punda for everyone to see. Our master took us in a cart to the execution and made us stand on the square and watch. He kept promising us the same fate if we defied him again. He was so superior. They had won. Once again we were mere slaves. And all our dear sons: dead."

"Oh Mai Yeye ..." Didi followed the story intensely, forgetting her own misery for a moment. "What happened then?" she asked.

"The Master brought us to the slave market, selling us one by one, splitting up whole families. Other plantations were doing the same. That is how they broke up all the rebellious pockets of slaves wanting to take revenge. Nobody went back to their own place. I just stood there and watched, waiting for my time to come. I could not let go of Mamawa. We did our best not to cry where the Master could see us. He was always gleeful if he could make somebody beg.

To our surprise he didn't sell Mamawa or me. He was smart. We were worth a lot because we were medicine women. So he hired us out to travel for weeks at a time to plantations to take care of the sick or wounded slaves that survived the fighting. But he never permitted us to go back to the plantation in the country where we came from. He kept us in Punda in his town house. I did not know that we would never see our huts again. I had to start all over again. I had only the clothes on my back.

I learned a hard lesson. From that day on, I never left my herbs behind me. Wherever I went I had a pouch with all I needed for an emergency. We all lost so much in that time. Mamawa never got to say good-bye to some of her sons."

Mai Yeye held Didi's hands.

"Don't ever think that I don't know what it means to hope for freedom or to resent this slavery. I know, but I am older now. I think I learned a lesson: if we are to be free, this freedom needs to come from God. The white man will never give us our freedom and we are not able to set ourselves free. We tried and have failed. If Tula could not do it for us then it is up to God.

Just like God set the Israelites free in the time of the Bible, so He will need to help us. I am praying that not one black man will lose his life fighting for our freedom. It was just too horrible to see all the bodies of our precious sons hanging from trees. I love Tula for what he did for us, what he tried to do even though he didn't succeed. I love him for trying. How much more do I love the Lord?

Do you understand, child? I have decided to be a slave for Christ. I figure, just like I can be a slave for the Master, I can be a slave for Christ. He didn't fail. Christ succeeded by defeating the devil. And one of these days he will come through for us and set us free.

Be encouraged for your baby. Your father was like Master Jacob but Sila didn't love you less did she? Or I? You are the most precious thing that has happened to us. We have each other; let us focus on that. Let us love this baby too."

Didi clung to her grandma. She held her tightly and could not say anything. Slowly her lips curled upwards in what could be a smile. In silence they hugged each other.

Later that day, Mai Yeye went to *Mefrou* Wilhelmina's room with a fresh cup of tea and a slice of apple pie. She didn't leave the room after serving her *Mefrou*. She stood motionless by the door waiting for *Mefrou* to acknowledge her.

"Yeye, why, what happened?"

"I ask permission to speak, my lady," Mai Yeye asked politely.

"Come closer and talk to me, Yeye. What is going on? Is it Didi, is it the baby? ... the father..?" Her voice trembled a little when she asked it.

"Yes, *Mefrou*, it is about Didi's baby. I know it is not my place to speak and I beg for forgiveness before I say what I am going to say. My word would never hold against another man's word, me being a black slave and all. But I want you to know that Didi got pregnant in this house."

Mefrou suppressed a scream. "I knew it, the bastard! I knew it. I saw that Didi was not behaving normally. She was skittish, sickly, depressed and not the happy child that I chose to take care of my baby."

Mefrou wrung her hands while she was speaking.

Mai Yeye shook her head. "No, *Mefrou*, this child is not a Jewish child. He has a chance to be born with blue eyes and blond hair. He will not have the brown curly hair from your husband."

Quickly she gave her *Mefrou* respect and left the room, full well knowing that what she just did was against all laws. Accusing a high-born man to be the father of a slave? Those words were surely enough for a death sentence for any slave. But Mai Yeye didn't care anymore. She needed to get *Mefrou* happy and eating again. Otherwise, this pregnancy would not go well. Her baby might die. And she didn't want the blame to fall on Didi.

Slowly, Mai Yeye walked to the porch where she knew her Master would sit with a whole bottle of port or jenever and stare into the night.

"Master Moron, can I speak freely to you?" she asked permission after she gave him a piece of the pie.

He nodded, absentmindedly.

"Master, I know that a slave should not speak out against one that is higher and mightier in station. And I only do so now because I trust my lord will remember all the care and love that my family has bestowed on your family. We would never do anything to harm you, my lord. You have treated us well."

Master Moron didn't want to hear a long speech. He waved his hands impatiently in the air. "Speak up woman, what do you know about this whole mess?"

"The child that is to be my grandson could be born with blue eyes and blond hair, Master," Mai Yeye said in a low voice.

Master Moron jumped up. "What? Where did she find somebody with blond hair and blue eyes to make a baby with?"

On that same moment the truth hit him. "My goodness! Did the bastard eat from my table and use one of my slaves? I wish ... I could lay hands on him, I would crush his ugly skinny throat with one hand! I would beat him up with my stick. That dog... that perverse dog... with such a young child like Didi."

Mai Yeye could not believe her ears. The Master wished to take a stick to another white man for the honor of his slave? She was astonished.

Her Master rushed past her, heading for his wife's room, certainly to make up with her!

Chapter Fifteen

It was Didi's day. Mai Yeye would act as her midwife while Sila stayed behind to care for *Mefrou* and the house. The delivery was not easy on Didi, but her youth and strong will got her through.

A tiny white baby girl was born. A gasp escaped Mai Yeye's throat when she saw how white the baby was. Immediately she turned the earlobe and looked behind it. Relieved, she noticed the color there was a coffee-with-lots-of-cream color. The child would not be too white.

Mai Yeye knew how difficult the life of a white slave girl was. She didn't wish that on any child. She raised the small bundle of a child in the air and said,

"God, we give you this child. Bless her and do not count to her the sins of her parents. Let hers be the generation that will experience freedom of slavery. Amen."

Didi stretched out her arms and received her child. With her grandmother's help she put the baby on her breast, and the baby suckled right away. Didi forgot in that split second all her pain, sadness, and hopeless feeling. She was filled with intense happiness at being a mother of such a perfect baby.

"Mai Yeye, she is perfect; will I learn to care for her?" Didi asked.

"Thank God she is perfect, Didi. You will need to love her; you are all she will ever have for a parent. It is up to you from this instant on to teach this child all she needs to know. You cannot look at her and feel resentment because of how she came to be. She needs all the help she can get to make it. Think on how your mother and I have loved you."

"Yes, Mai Yeye, I am happy she is not too white. I was afraid she would be a white slave."

"She comes into a world that is divided by color. She needs to be white to count. But because she is a slave she needs to be black to survive the horrible life of a light-skinned slave. But now, because she is a black girl, people will look down on her and assume she isn't intelligent. It is up to us to help her develop and be confident in her skills as the next generation medicine woman in our family. Just like we need to teach her medicine, we need to teach her to be a good slave. We want her to stay in the house and be a house slave. You don't want your daughter to do back-breaking work in the fields, do you?"

Didi nodded. She understood the seriousness of the situation. Then she said,

"I guess I will stay in the house with you and Mai Sila now. Bois hasn't come over for months." Didi looked sad.

"I am sorry it didn't work out with Bois. He is a good boy. Someday another person will come and ask you, and you will build a life then. Thank God, Master Moron doesn't give house slaves to the men to produce babies. You will have plenty of time to decide if you want to hold hands again or not. For now, your baby is your main responsibility."

Didi held her grandmother's hand and promised to take good care of the baby. They prayed together.

The door of their hut flew open and Mai Sila rushed in.

"How is she, Mai?" she asked breathlessly. "*Mefrou* kept me, and I could not come sooner."

She reached over and touched the baby. "A girl," she said. Then, just as Mai Yeye had done, she turned the earlobe of the baby.

"Nice milk chocolate girl," she said, smiling, trying to make her words light-hearted. But Didi could see her relief.

"What is her name?" Mai Sila asked next.

Mai Yeye and Didi looked at each other and laughed.

"We talked about so much and we prayed, but we forgot to choose a name," Mai Yeye said.

"Mimina," Didi said in a clear voice. "Her name will be Mimina."

"Mimina?" Mai Sila was testing the name. "Why Mimina? Why not a name from the Bible stories that we know? Or an African name?"

"Just like Mimina from the island of Bonaire. She was a slave. She lived in Kunuku Rincon. She escaped and made it to Venezuela. She worked there as a free person and had financial stability," Didi said. "I pray and hope that my daughter will be free one day too."

Mai Sila and Mai Yeye understood her feelings and agreed to the name.

Didi continued, "I prayed for a baby girl. It is much easier for me to care for a girl. We can keep her in the house. If the Master permits it, we can teach her to become a house slave. And she can become a medicine woman just like us. She will make it in the world when she is free."

Didi stayed in her room with the baby until she was ready to work again. Then she brought the baby for her *Mefrou* to see. *Mefrou* Wilhelmina took the child from her and opened the blanket—an old one from Chris—that the baby was wrapped in. She took a long time to look the baby over. Didi stood still and waited. Finally, *Mefrou* said,

"Take good care of her, Didi, she is a spunky one. She will be beautiful. I am happy for you that she doesn't have blue eyes."

Master Moron entered the room and peeked at the baby.

"Well done, Didi," he said and walked back out the door. Then he put his head back in and said, "You and your family have been faithful to us. I will not sell your baby. Keep her and train her to serve us as you do. She will be the slave of the baby we are expecting now. If she stays here with us, she will be safe with that white color."

From that day on, Didi was mother to both Chris and Mimina.

Le Docteur was called and Mai Yeye started preparing. The baby was expected any time now. Prayers were being sent to heaven continually for the health of *Mefrou* and her new baby.

Mai Sila had been fanning *Mefrou* the whole morning, not daring to let someone else do that job. She was observing *Mefrou*, who was complaining of a heavy headache and of the heat. Master Moron was pacing the floor and threw worried glances at his wife. Every now and then he looked out of the window. Where was Le Docteur?

With her hands, *Mefrou* indicated for the Master to come closer. With a trembling voice she said, "Something is wrong, I don't feel good. Call Mai Yeye and let her help me. Do not wait for Le Docteur."

Master Moron brought his face even closer to *Mefrou* and turned his back to Mai Sila. In a very low voice he said, "I see that you are not doing well. But I cannot let two slaves deliver our baby. They don't know anything about delivering our babies. They only know how to work with slaves."

"Remember how good they were when Chris was born?" *Mefrou* pleaded.

"I know...I know, even Le Docteur was impressed that they knew so much. But this time it is different. You are not doing well."

Mefrou closed her eyes and held on tightly to her husband while she waited for another pain wave to subside. "Please, my love, trust me in this. They know how to be around sick people and I am sick. I cannot do this on my own. Please call Yeye and let her help me. If Le Docteur arrives he can take over from there."

Master Moron ran his fingers through his hair and walked over to the window, where he looked outside again.

He heard a loud shriek and, alarmed, he turned around to find his wife doubled over in pain. Her face was red and hot, her eyes wide open, panicked. Her face looked swollen.

He looked over at Mai Sila and their eyes met for a short moment before she lowered hers in submission. But did he see a pleading look? In a split second Master Moron made a decision. "Sila, give me that fan and go tell Yeye to come help *Mefrou* with her delivery."

Mai Yeye was standing in the corridor with a canister full of what she thought was needed. She was in prayer.

"Mai, the Master sent for you, *Mefrou* Wilhelmina is not doing well."

"I was expecting this. What do you think? Is it the fever in the head?"

"It looks like it, Mai."

"Quick, run and get Didi. Come back with the hot water. I have Ruby in the kitchen; she can watch the children for now. I will go in and check on *Mefrou*."

Master Moron looked up, surprised when the door of the room opened softly after less than a minute. His slave came in, clearly prepared for this situation.

Mai Yeye leaned over *Mefrou* and touched her head and hands. She opened the duvet and inspected her legs. She looked up to the Master and made a sign with her eyes to follow her outside. There she spoke clearly, saying, "Master, I think *Mefrou* has fever in her head. I have seen this before in some slave women. It is very dangerous. There are some things we can do but I don't know if it will help and I need your permission."

"Do what you can, Yeye." The Master's face was white and his eyes skittish. "What do you need? Can I help?"

The serious situation made both of them forget the normal master-slave relationship. Master Moron accepted Mai Yeye's authority without questioning it.

"Can you send for Fito? I think I need ice. I sent Sila for Didi. I need the help of them both."

Not long after that all three medicine women were in *Mefrou*'s room. Master Moron came back and made it clear that he was not leaving his wife, even though it was not customary for men to be in the delivery room.

Didi took over the fanning. Mai Sila was cleaning some karpata leaves and mixing them with coconut oil. They bound that mixture to *Mefrou*'s head to cool her down and lower the fever. Then Sila poured some coconut oil on *Mefrou*'s head and massaged it into the scalp.

Mai Yeye had a portion of shredded fresh potatoes and she made a poultice, which she bound under the patient's feet.

Fito arrived just then with a whole block of ice. The women received the heavy block of ice from Fito and put it in the bathtub. They poured a little water over the ice and put a blanket and some towels in the water. Mai Sila and Mai Yeye were working quickly and silently together. Sometimes they stopped working to comfort *Mefrou* when she had a painful contraction. *Mefrou* was whimpering, holding her head with two hands.

"*Mefrou*," Mai Yeye said when the blankets and the towels were ready. "I am going to put some very cold and wet towels over you to help you cool down. It will be cold for you but it will help you. Do you understand me?"

Mefrou could not answer, her eyes were glassy and her head kept moving from left to right. She didn't give any sign that she was hearing what Yeye was saying. Mai Yeye looked up to her Master for his permission and received a nod.

Mai Sila gave Didi a sign and all three of them took up a side of the blanket and put it over *Mefrou*, folding her completely in the cold, wet blanket. Mai Yeye used the towel to fold over *Mefrou*'s head and neck, leaving only her face uncovered. All three of the women were praying under their breath, realizing full well that the life of their *Mefrou* was in their hands.

When the towel became drier, Mai Sila changed it and applied another cold one. They wet a second blanket and changed the wet blanket between two contractions. The clock ticked the minutes away. It felt like hours, but it might have been only ten minutes.

"Norbert, are you here?" *Mefrou* asked unexpectedly, uttering her first intelligible word in the last hour.

"*Mefrou* is asking for you, Master," Mai Yeye said, while she signaled Sila and Didi to move to the far end of the room to give the couple privacy.

Master Moron held his wife's hands. Tears fell on them.

"I feel much better, Norbert," *Mefrou* announced. "I feel cool again. For a moment there, I was so hot that I felt like my head was going to explode. My headache is gone too."

Master Moron couldn't talk. He held his wife tightly and helped her through another contraction. She fell asleep and Master Moron signaled the women to take over. They removed the wet towels from *Mefrou* and dried her off, changing the wet bed sheets and her wet undergarment. Master took a chair next to his wife and soothed her through some contractions.

Mai Yeye kept track of the contractions and noticed that the time was approaching rapidly. She made a mental note of all that she needed and saw that it was all there, laid out awaiting the time it would be needed.

Mai Yeye indicated to the Master that the time was soon and he gave them some space to work. Mai Sila helped Mai Yeye position *Mefrou* better. And the work began. Mai Yeye was coaching *Mefrou* with a soothing voice.

While they had all forgotten to wait for Le Docteur, the good man was ushered in with the utmost haste by Ruby. He brought with him his nurse, another one this time. With a demanding tone, he began calling for some items, only to find out that all was laid out and ready for him to use.

"Okay, ladies," he said, directing himself to the medicine women, "you can go outside now and wait for me. I will take over from here." And to the Master he said, "All is well, Moron; take a glass of port in the library and I will send for you when your baby is born."

None of them moved. Master Moron took a step closer to his wife. Mai Yeye and Mai Sila acted as if they didn't hear the doctor.

Before the situation could go on any further, *Mefrou* shrieked and the baby arrived. Mai Yeye, who was the closest, received the baby right away. With expertise, she turned the baby upside down, opened her mouth to check it out, cleaned her mouth, blew in her face and gave the baby a firm slap on her small behind. The baby sputtered a little but then gave a clear cry. She was tiny and almost colorless. Mai Sila, Mai Yeye, and Didi gave a loud yell of victory when the baby cried.

Mefrou was stretching her neck to see. "Yeye, is the baby okay? Let me see," she said in a feeble voice.

"She has everything, *Mefrou*: ten toes, two hands and ten fingers. Look!" Proudly, Mai Yeye held the baby for her *Mefrou* to see. "Let me clean her up and you can have her." She gave the baby to Mai Sila to wash her and salve her with a salt ointment.

Mai Yeye swore by her salt ointment. "It takes the sickness away," she claimed.

Le Docteur observed the whole situation. He saw how Mai Yeye was putting pressure on the belly of *Mefrou*, trying to stop the bleeding. Didi stopped her fanning and was chipping ice, which they used to make a cold compress.

Mai Yeye had a black tea prepared that she gave *Mefrou* to drink. It was used to stop the bleeding. The nurse, who felt left out, hurried to take the baby from Mai Sila. Mai Yeye signaled Sila with her eyes to give the baby to the nurse now. The nurse received the baby and put her to nurse on her mother.

Le Docteur was examining *Mefrou*. He noticed that the blood stream was diminishing and eventually stopped. Mai Yeye also saw this and she let out a soft breath. All was well.

Quietly, the three slaves cleaned the room up and left, leaving a healthy baby and a happy *Mefrou* behind.

Chapter Sixteen

In the kitchen, Didi used hot water to wash the dirty sheets. Mai Yeye took care of all the bowls they had used, and Mai Sila prepared the refreshment to serve. She poured a glass of port for the Master and brewed some tea. A plate of delicate sandwiches was ready. She carried it to the porch to be ready for the Master when he came out.

She knocked on the door of the sleeping room and asked for permission to speak. With her head and eyes cast down she said, "I can stay with *Mefrou* if you and the nurse would like to eat and drink something. It is ready on the porch."

"These slaves are very competent, Moron," Le Docteur complimented his friend.

"Thank God for them, Docteur. You would not have gotten anything from me. I forgot to eat and to drink myself, and I certainly would have forgotten that you and your nurse might be hungry and thirsty after your ride from town and then the delivery."

Turning to Sila he said, "We will come take those refreshments, Sila, but I do not want tea. I think I need something stronger for now. Don't you think I deserve it?"

Sila smiled and did not answer. The Master would notice soon enough that his "something stronger" was there to accommodate him.

"Can I stay with *Mefrou* and the baby?" she asked.

The Master nodded. Just as he turned to walk away, he noticed something else in her hand.

"What do you have there, Sila?" he asked.

"It is a small pouch Mai Yeye sewed for the baby. See? With these straps we could tie it easily on *Mefrou* so she could walk her baby with her hands free. It is something Mai Yeye thought would help, *Mefrou*. We used the softest cotton from an old blanket from Chris, Master. It will not hurt the baby."

Master Moron nodded and walked away, pensive. Le Docteur also observed, and he commented, "Moron, you have done a good job training these women. Again, I am really impressed. They saved your wife's life."

Master Moron quietly smoked his cigar. He said honestly, "I have nothing to do with the training of these women. I am in the fields working the whole day or in Punda doing business. I didn't even know these women before I came to live on this plantation. And even when I came to live here, I never saw them or spoke with them. They have a way of bringing in my food and drinks just when I need them, as they have done now for you too. And they keep the house running. My wife is mostly in bed, as you know. So she cannot train them either. I noticed them the first time when they helped with my son and now again with the delivery of my daughter."

"You need to sell me one. I need such a capable midwife. Please Moron, you promised last time."

"I did no such thing. I did not promise. But I thought about it. I looked for their paperwork to know what they were bought for to establish a price. The strange thing is that I cannot find their paperwork. I have the property papers from all the field slaves, even from the old house slaves, but not for the three medicine women. And you know without proof of ownership I cannot sell a slave. I asked my wife and she said that her father bought them quite unexpectedly from a man in town. I think I will need to write to my father-in-law to ask him for their paperwork."

"Yes, please, Moron, look for the paperwork and sell me one of these capable women. I think I would rather have the older one, what is her name? Yeye? She seems very capable. But she might be too old to help me with all the traveling we do. I prefer the young one. I might be able to teach her something the rich white ladies expect. They really need pampering."

Neither of the men realized Mai Sila was just coming up to the porch. She overheard the last comment, how Le Docteur offered to buy one of them. She stopped in her tracks. Not again. Please God, not again. A pitiful sound escaped her throat. When will this stop: these threats of being sold, away from the family? Without calling the Master as her *Mefrou* had asked, she turned and walked to the kitchen.

She didn't hear her Master turn down Le Docteur as politely as possible. When Mai Sila arrived in the kitchen, the news hit like a bomb. Mai Yeye had tears in her eyes. Anxiously, Didi hugged them both.

On the porch, leaning back in his comfortable porch chair, Master Moron said, "You know, Docteur, they are very united as a family. They work well together. They are always there to help my family. Yeye is the grandmother, Sila is her daughter, Didi is her daughter, and they have a baby. She is a newborn. I could not sell her mother from her. She is not weaned yet. With my feeble wife and a new baby in the house, I need all the help I can get."

Le Docteur nodded. "Are you not too soft on these people? After all, they are just slaves. Somebody else can take care of that baby, I am sure. When you feel ready to sell one, please give me the first choice. I will buy one from you any day." After taking a sip of his port he said, "Every plantation I visit needs a medicine woman, and you have three. It is just not acceptable."

Master Moron laughed out loud. "I am lucky, I know."

"Write your father-in-law quickly. You need to have the proof of ownership in your hands to claim these women as yours and to be able to sell them."

Master Moron nodded.

Le Docteur asked him, "May I call Mai Yeye to ask her what she put in that black tea she gave your wife to stop the bleeding? I never saw such severe bleeding stop so quickly."

But Master Moron didn't want his slaves to get more attention from Le Docteur. He said, "They are very busy right now. They take care of this family, the new baby, my sick wife, and the cooking for us. I don't think we should take more time from them."

Mefrou rang the bell and Didi went to her. *Mefrou* wanted to see the baby again, and she wanted to speak with her husband. Didi called him and went back to fan *Mefrou*.

"Norbert, we have a girl," *Mefrou* said with a small voice. "Just like I wanted."

Her husband hugged her and took a good look at the baby that was now dressed in white ruffles.

"Didi, can you bring Chris now, so he can meet his sister?" the Master asked.

Didi walked to the hut of Willie and found Chris playing in a corner with Willie's teenage daughter. Baby Mimina was sleeping on a mat in the dark. As soon as Didi saw her daughter, her breast came to life and filled with milk. Carefully Didi picked up the baby and quickly fed her.

Chris kept chattering, telling his Yaya all that occurred when he was playing in the unfamiliar surroundings. Didi held him tightly by his arm, leading him back to his mother and father before he could disappear again, chasing a cat or chicken. He loved the chickens that were walking around the yard. His long thin face looked upwards with great love and adoration for his Yaya. He didn't stop talking.

Didi looked lovingly at him as well. He was not a handsome boy. His face was too long, his ears stood out, and his eyes were too close to each other. No grace there. But Didi loved that small white boy with the same love she had for Mimina. He was her boy, no questions asked.

Chris was excited to hear that he had a sister. When he came into the room, he ran to the baby. *Mefrou* Wilhelmina woke up. The baby was sleeping next to her.

"The baby is here, Chris, go wash your hands and come meet your sister. Her name is Miriam Josefina Moron."

From that day on, Didi was Yaya of both the children of her *Mefrou* and her own baby. They were always together. Didi would carry one baby in one arm and the other in the other arm, displaying one brown and one white child.

When, after just two months, *Mefrou's* milk dried up, Didi fed both children for almost the whole year. The children grew up as brothers and sisters, playing together and learning together.

Mefrou never recovered from her illness and stayed in bed or in her room most of the time. When the children were playing in the yard, she would open her windows and wave to them, blowing kisses and encouraging them. The children learned to look up at the windows and call out for her.

In the year that both girls had their fourth birthdays, the old Fito of the plantation died. This incident left the slaves in uncertainty for some time. The old Fito was a harsh man and he was not easy to please, but the slaves were used to him and knew how to dodge him. Getting a new Fito meant learning a new man's ways. And it could mean enduring many more hardships and corporal punishments. The prayer group was very active.

So it was that the Master brought one of his Fitos from Punda to manage his plantation. From the beginning, it was clear that this Fito was much easier to work with than the deceased one had been. He was strict with the rules but didn't resort to inhuman beatings. The most important thing he didn't do was to look at the women or young girls with desire. He quickly won over the men because of this. None of them wanted to share their women with him or the Master.

Mai Yeye called him into the kitchen and explained to him how the prayer group came together before or after work.

"Does the Master know this, Yeye?" he asked, not impolitely.

"No, we never told him, but since it is before work and on Sundays, it doesn't interfere with our work. The other Fito laughed at us, but he didn't interfere. Why don't you come this weekend and check it out for yourself? If you find anything that you feel is not good, you can tell the Master then."

Fito visited and met the prayer group. After that first time he kept visiting. He liked Mai Sila and came by uninvited to the kitchen to have some coffee with her. She didn't know what to do with the attention of a man, only having known Master Jan's attention.

He talked with Mai Yeye about his feelings for Sila. But Mai Yeye could not help him. Sila could not trust any man. She was not accepting his advances.

It went on for many months until Fito decided to talk with Master Moron, asking permission to share a hut together.

Master Moron was surprised with the development. He always thought about the medicine women as house slaves without a personal life. Confronted with this question, he gave the Fito permission before asking Sila her wishes.

Both Mai Yeye and Mai Sila were taken aback by the decision of the Master that the Fito would move in the room under the house with Sila.

Mai Sila said to him when he came for coffee the next day, "I cannot move in. I am a follower of Christ, and I need to be married."

"I will marry you any day, my love." Fito looked into her eyes and saw her doubt. "I will speak with

Papa Bubu and we could jump the broom this Sunday if you want. My room is ten steps from your mother's room. It is not as if you are moving away. I just want to have you for myself."

"I need to talk with my mother first. I cannot marry you this Sunday."

Fito smiled broadly, his white teeth showing in his big round black face. "Any Sunday will do for me, my love. I will wait faithfully for you to talk with whosoever you want. In the meantime, I will prepare our room. I have some skills in working wood, so I will ask the boys to help me fell a tree to make you a nice table and some chairs. Maybe your mother wants to make us a wide mattress?"

Sila's face flamed hot when he referred to a cozy room with a big mattress. She turned her back on him and tried to get herself under control.

Soon the big day arrived, and Sila left the room she had shared with her mother and daughter for so long and moved in with Fito. The whole prayer group blessed them. Mai Yeye cried. Didi cried. Even little Mimina cried just because her whole family was crying.

It turned out that Fito was a good husband for Sila and that he didn't take Sila away from her mother and family. Actually, he was very fond of the family and joined them wholeheartedly. Every day after work he would sit with the family under the tamarind tree and offered his manly input in the female environment. They got used to relying on Fito's opinion.

Sila had landed herself a good man.

Chapter Seventeen

Didi took on most of the work of collecting and drying leaves that Mai Yeye had done for so long. It was easy for her, being so young, to roam the woods with her three charges playing along. She was muscular and lean from all her work. She had an attractive body with wide hips. She walked with a rhythmic swing. Sometimes she used the quiet walks to think about how her life could have been.

From the day Bois and his family bought their freedom, she never heard from him again, and she learned to have peace with the situation. She heard from Fito that the family was living in Punda and was scraping by to survive. Life was not easy for slaves, and not easy for free blacks either. They remained black and poor even when they were free. Didi was happy for Bois that he was a free man. She knew he would find his way. She could not have been married with a free man—that was for sure.

Didi focused more and more on training Mimina, who at four years old already knew how to pick leaves and bring them back for Mai Yeye to cook. The house chores had been delegated mostly to Ruby, who was properly trained by Mai Sila. Ruby didn't live in the Big House but walked to her hut after the work was done at night. In the early morning, she would walk back to the kitchen where she would help Didi with the wash. With two active kids and *Mefrou* Wilhelmina in bed, they had a lot to wash. The bed sheets were big, and it took two to hang them.

Didi tried to do all her heavy work in the morning before the kids woke up. So she started at four o'clock, hauled water, and made the fire. On special days, she prepared to make coconut oil. The plantation went through a lot of coconut oil each week, and it was up to Didi to see that there was a good supply. They also started selling some of the oil to people who requested it, and Fito took the small bottles to sell in Punda. The coconut oil with herbs turned out to be the favorite in town, and Didi made a double batch of that. That was a special recipe from Mai Yeye handed down from Mamawa.

Sila, Didi, and Yeye used the same oil for healing. They started experimenting with using it for shortness of breath because Mai Yeye thought that heart problems caused people to be out of breath. She also used it for coughs and for pain in the breast. She made the patients drink one spoon of coconut oil daily. Mai Yeye always had a bottle of oil with her in case somebody had a fever. Didi used it for constipation, and Mai Sila made an ointment out of it for dry or irritated skin. Even *Mefrou* used the face ointment. The biggest demand for the oil came from the Big House, where they used it to light the lamps.

On other days, Didi got up early to make soap to keep the plantation well supplied. They made only enough soap for the Big House and personal use, not for the field slaves.

When Chris turned six years old, *Mefrou* sent for a tutor to teach him. It saddened Didi to see 'her son' leave her daily care. She could only glimpse Chris at the dining table now. The tutor took care of him, planning his day and teaching him. Chris attended his classes in the loft, which had been transformed into a classroom. He was in classes the whole morning, and after lunch his tutor kept him busy riding horses, swimming, or going to town to visit a museum.

The tutor was a serious-looking, stocky young man, dressed in a formal black suit. He never laughed or made jokes. When Chris came running to Didi, the tutor reprimanded him sharply. "You are a big boy now, Chris. You cannot be hugging a black lady like that. She is your slave. You are the Master."

Chris's lips trembled, but he walked away after throwing Didi an apologetic glance. He didn't come close after that, but sometimes Didi would see him standing in the loft looking down on them when she was in the yard with the girls. That is why she decided not to play with the girls in the yard when he was upstairs. He looked down so longingly and seemed to be so lonely up there. The tutor was irritated by Chris's persistence in wanting to visit his Yaya. He talked with the Master and *Mefrou*, and they instructed Didi that from that day on she was to call Baby Chris "Master Chris" and abstain from any conversation or direct contact with him.

When he turned eight years old, his tutor started talking with his parents about sending him to Europe to finish his education. Chris had a love for reading and spent all his time reading in his room or the classroom. The tutor thought he was ready for a formal education. *Mefrou* cried and begged her husband not to send him away, but to no avail. The best thing for Chris was to get him away from all these women and get him into a learning environment, his tutor argued—and his arguments won out over *Mefrou*'s tears. Master Moron spent more and more of his time in Punda tending to his more profitable enterprises. He was not going to let a sickly wife and some slave women determine the future of his son. At nine years of age, Chris sailed for Europe, and life continued on the plantation without him.

With the departure of Chris, *Mefrou*'s health deteriorated and she never left her room anymore. Didi also mourned her 'son' Chris. At least she got to keep the two girls.

The girls didn't mind Chris's leaving so much. For years they were not allowed to play with him, and they saw him only from afar. His departure didn't interfere with their games. Since Miriam was a thin, sickly child, Master Moron didn't order a tutor for her. She was going to receive classes from a teacher who would come twice a week to instruct her.

Didi was excited. Miriam would learn how to read and write. Maybe—just maybe—the Master would allow Mimina to learn too. Wouldn't that be grand? Didi prayed and prayed about her silent plan, and one day after fanning *Mefrou*, she dared to bring it up.

"*Mefrou*, would you permit Mimina to be in the classes with Miriam when the teacher gives classes?"

Mefrou was taken by surprise. "But Didi, a slave taking reading and writing classes? Isn't that too difficult for the poor child?"

"She is exactly the same age as Miriam, *Mefrou*," Didi said respectfully.

"If you think she would like to...if she can...if it is not a strain for her...I guess I am all right with it then," *Mefrou* said, a little uncertain about everything.

When she told her husband about the new plans, she was surprised at his reaction. "How could you permit that, Wilhelmina? Mimina is a slave. She doesn't need to read or write. She needs to cook and clean."

A flustered *Mefrou* Wilhelmina started dabbing her eyes. "Norbert, these people care for me. They feel like family to me. I could not say no. Do you have any idea how many hours Didi is in here fanning me? I would not like her to have a hostile attitude against me just for some stupid classes."

"Mimina wouldn't be able to understand reading and writing anyway, Wilhelmina. These people are from Africa, for God's sake."

"Norbert, if Mimina doesn't understand the classes, all the better. At least she will have tried and found that it proved difficult. At least it is not me saying no to Didi."

"There is nothing wrong saying no to your slave. They are here to serve you and not the other way around."

"That might be true when you are healthy but not when you depend on them to feed you, to change you, or to support you in a chair. If it was up to me, I would have given them their freedom." *Mefrou* wept openly now. "They surely behave more humanely than many upright citizens that I know whose only virtue is that they are white."

Master Moron looked uncomfortable. Any mention of the slave women being set free made him recoil. He remembered the letter he received from Master Pe from the Netherlands, in which he explained the conditions under which the slaves came to the plantation. He also reasoned that the slaves were to be set free since their old Master Jan and his wife Victoria died without having children, and the property was sold and sent to a distant relative in Australia. There was no one to claim the women as theirs. There were no slave documents for them. Master Pe suggested that Moron set them free and hire them as paid workers.

Master Moron hid that letter and never mentioned it again. How was he to travel to Punda and do business if his wife was so sick in bed? He needed those women to care for his child, home, and wife.

He promised himself to set the women free as soon as his wife was well enough to care for her children and the home. Until then he needed them.

Master Moron walked to his wife and embraced her. "I am sorry I was so inconsiderate with you," he murmured in her ear. "I guess there is no harm in Mimina learning to read and write. You were right. Let's do it."

The other person who was not happy with the arrangement was the teacher. She learned about her special student only after accepting a good amount of cash from Master Moron and signing the papers. She could not turn the job down now.

During the first lesson, she instructed her two pupils about the class rules. Mimina was to sit in the back of the class and was never to say, ask, or comment on anything. She could only listen. Also, she was there to serve both the teacher and Miriam in case they needed a glass of water or a forgotten book.

Mimina, with her happy disposition, didn't question the rule. From the time she was very young, she was instructed by her mother that she was to be the personal slave of Miriam. She loved Miriam and didn't mind doing anything for her.

Miriam and Mimina proved to be intelligent children. With no effort at all, they learned to read and to write. *Mefrou* was pleased with the work and instructed the teacher to come four times a week. The children were also instructed in history, geography, and biology. When they both turned ten, the teacher instructed them in table manners, the classics, dance, and recitation of poetry.

Mai Yeye and Mai Sila were very proud of their grandchild. She was learning. She was intelligent. She was able to read the Bible. They bragged to each other about all the virtues of Mimina.

Didi sat under the tamarind tree and heard her daughter recite a poem in high Dutch. Didi, who initially wanted her daughter to learn to read and to write, was not so sure about the developments. She shook her head. What was going to happen with them? She wanted her daughter to be prepared in case they were freed, but she was afraid Mimina would not make a good slave since she knew so much from the other world. When Didi tried to share her concerns with her family, she met with a stone wall. Neither her mother nor grandmother shared those concerns. Even Fito, usually the conservative one, approved.

"God knows what He does, child." Mai Yeye touched Didi softly. "Your job is to teach Mimina how to be a good medicine woman and how to keep a house. If He wants to teach our Mimina how to behave like white people, He has a plan for her. So do not fret."

Didi brought the situation to God and let it rest.

Chapter Eighteen

Mimina and Miriam grew up together as close as cousins. They followed each other all day long. Where Mimina was, Miriam went. Where Miriam was, Mimina went. They did all their homework together and played with the dolls Miriam got for her birthdays. Mimina wore all of Miriam's used clothes.

Mimina was a happy child. She never resented being Miriam's servant. She helped her mother serve at the table and made sure to give Miriam the choicest servings and the biggest slices of chocolate dessert. Mimina lived life with a big smile and had nothing to worry about. Miriam would playfully 'order' her to go to the kitchen and bake a cake for her. Mimina brought Miriam's requests to her mom and grandma. When the cake was ready, Miriam would take it to the woods and the two of them would eat it and laugh together. They would jump rope, play ball, make dolls out of straw and old material, and do homework together.

Even though Mimina was made to sit in the back seat in her classes, she managed to learn everything the teacher taught them. She "helped" Miriam with her homework and, in the last years of their formal education, she did all of Miriam's homework. The teacher never knew.

When they both turned twelve, they outgrew some of their childish games, but they still could be found sitting on the porch, talking, laughing, or sewing together. If it was up to the teacher, they would not be allowed to spend so much time together anymore. She thought Miriam should be playing with her own kind now that she was a young lady.

The teacher regularly took Miriam to Punda to see plays or to shop for clothes. Sometimes they would stay in Punda for days at a time, visiting Master Moron's family and friends there. Mimina was not welcome. When Miriam arrived home, she brought many stories and beautiful gowns with her.

At the insistence of the teacher, *Mefrou* sent out invitations for girls from other plantations to come and visit Miriam. Soon Miriam didn't want to go out into the sunshine anymore. She was "watching her complexion," she said. Whenever she did go outside, she used a parasol, and sometimes Mimina was the one who carried it for her.

How Mimina wished they could go in the woods again, swim in the pond—the one they were not allowed to swim in but did anyway—and play hide and seek as they did when they were younger.

These days, Mimina was busier in the house, having taken on many chores from Didi, who was helping Mai Yeye more and more. Didi took her responsibility of instructing Mimina very seriously, and before Mimina turned thirteen, she knew how to treat all minor illnesses and wounds. She was accompanying Mai Sila and Didi to the slave huts to prepare women for delivering their babies. Didi taught her everything she knew about the reproductive cycle of life.

Over and over, Didi instructed her how to behave to not attract attention from any man. "Never trust any man, Mimina. Be very careful. Your father looked nice, he had many friends, he was an important man in the society, but he did this to me."

"Why can a white man force a black woman to do such things?" Mimina didn't understand. "Shouldn't somebody say something about it?"

"Who will, girl? Who is going to say something? Who knows? A black slave can never say anything against a white man. That is punishable with lashes and sometimes even death. There is no white voice to speak for us. That is the way things are in our society. Slaves don't count. We are here for our Masters and they can do whatever they want. If we escape, they can send dogs after us, capture us, and let Bomba finish us. You'd better understand that early. There is no justice in this world, so do not think life will be any different for you. You pray and keep out of trouble, that is all you can do."

Mimina was duly impressed. She determined right there, never to trust white males and not to expose herself to them. With Didi's help, that was easy. As soon as Master Moron brought somebody from Punda, she sent Mimina on a long errand collecting leaves or helping somebody in the slave huts. Mimina was not allowed inside the house to see or meet any white male.

Her mother told her regularly, "You cannot trust anybody, girl, neither white nor black. Make sure you are in our house before it is dark outside. Always stay with one of us. Do not wander alone too far. Do not smile and joke with the young boys or men in the fields. Just be polite. You don't want them to understand your friendliness as an invitation."

The only time Mimina was to serve white guests was when Miriam demanded Mimina to serve at her tea parties.

The tea parties Miriam hosted usually included four or five friends. She loved to show Mimina off to her friends. She had seen in the other homes how her new friends treated their servants and she was trying to do the same to impress them. She demanded things from Mimina she had never called for before. Mimina did all her chores quickly and with a smile. Miriam's new friends were properly impressed. None of them had a medicine woman as their personal slave.

"You are so lucky," one of the girls named Lauren said. "We only have two old bags as house slaves. When I ring for them, it takes hours for them to drag their feet and come. But you have a quick young slave and she is a medicine woman. Wow."

"And she is not so ugly as our slaves; you should see mine," Suzy from Plantation Rio Lindo added. "I have a personal slave, I need one. With this long hair and all those buttons that the new fashions require, I could not survive without Adidi. Even her name is silly... and she is so ugly. Her big, fat black face just stares at me. She does all that I tell her to do, though." She smiled maliciously. "I taught her to obey me."

The conversation drifted from bad slaves to tea parties and invitations for dances. Miriam had not been to a dance, since she was not yet fifteen. She was full of questions and wanted to hear all about the dances.

"You will need to have new dresses," Laureen pointed out, staring at Miriam's flat bosom. Miriam was tall and thin. Her breasts started growing but then stopped, leaving her with an awkward size. Her hair was pale and lifeless. With all of this, plus her long face and broad lips, she was not a pretty girl.

Miriam felt uncomfortable under her gaze and tried to laugh it off. "My daddy will buy me whatever I ask him," she said, knowing full well that Laureen's dad could not do that. If she didn't even have a personal slave, and if they only could have two old slaves in their house, then Miriam knew how the situation was for Laureen.

"I will go to Punda with Adam when he goes to bring produce next week, and I will get me some dresses," she boasted, and the battle was over. None of the other girls could command a driver to bring them to Punda just to buy dresses.

Mai Yeye had been such a strong pillar in all their lives that they could not imagine life without her. But on a Monday morning, without warning, Mai Yeye didn't wake up. She died without seeing the freedom she had prayed for her whole life.

It was a big setback for many people. Fito sent for Adam right away and he set in motion the customary rituals associated with a slave's death. Others went up on the highest point of the plantation and, for hours, sounded the horn that announced the death of beloved Mai Yeye.

Mimina was working in the Big House when she heard the horn's faint sound. She could remember the day that horn was made. Fito brought home a steer's horn. When he sawed off a piece of it and made two holes in it, it became a useful instrument. Mimina remembered well how he did that as he sat under the tamarind tree. Fito used his horn every day to call the slaves to the field or back to their huts. He could speak into the horn, using it to amplify his voice so it was loud enough for all to hear. Mai Yeye was there that night. She was sewing something. They were all laughing and talking. Now it was that same horn that announced her death.

That night, under the cover of darkness, different free black people came to pay their last respects to Mai Yeye. Fitos from neighboring plantations also received permission to come and say their good-byes. Yeye had been a medicine woman for many slaves and had helped countless children come into this world. These people were coming to honor a woman who had been a part of their lives. She was buried that very night, as was the custom.

The next day, *Mefrou* sent for Sila, Didi, and Mimina. "I am sorry about Yeye," *Mefrou* said to Mimina. "I thought I would die before she did. But I guess I am younger than she was."

"Thank you, *Mefrou*," replied Mimina.

"I have decided that Mimina and Didi should take over the house chores and you, Sila, should go to the kitchen and take over Mai Yeye's work."

The medicine women mourned for days.

For Mimina, her great-grandmother's death meant that all her free time was gone and so was her childhood. No more classes with Miriam or time spent sewing. She would be completely occupied with her chores, especially since *Mefrou* Wilhelmina was so fragile. She needed continual help and that required a lot of Didi's time, leaving Mimina with most of the chores.

"Call Didi for me please, tell her that I am not feeling well," *Mefrou* Wilhelmina requested. "And call Adam and tell him to go to town to fetch my husband. I need him here."

In the middle of the night, Master Moron arrived and stayed home for the whole week with his ailing wife. She was in tears. "Norbert, Mai Yeye died. I am going to die, and my baby Miriam is going to be fifteen. Please send for Chris," she begged him. "I am going to die and I haven't seen my son in years. My father passed away and I could not go to Europe to be with my mother. I want my son now." She was completely overstressed.

Le Docteur came from Punda and prescribed some medicine with a calming effect. Master Moron stayed until she was feeling better and promised to organize a nice 15th birthday party for Miriam.

And he did just that. He ordered the front of the plantation to be painted in a bright new yellow color. The slaves were put to work. The yard in front of the plantation was tended and the big sitting room was converted into a party room. Mai Sila, Didi, and Mimina were cooking and baking for days—no, weeks. The best of the best was brought into the house to make this party worthy of the only daughter of the house, who was coming of age. The invitations were hand-delivered. *Mefrou* wanted to have input in the decision about what Miriam was to wear, so she sent for a seamstress from Punda.

Miriam was excited and could talk about nothing but her upcoming party. Even *Mefrou* looked better in the midst of all the excitement.

On the day of the party, Didi, her mother, and her daughter got up at 4 o'clock. They filled the oil lamps and placed them around strategically in the party room. The decorations had already been finished by the company that Master Moron brought in from Punda. In lovely silver vases, sunny yellow flowers lit up the room and emitted a pleasing fragrance.

Mai Sila hastened to the kitchen where twenty slaves arrived around five o'clock to start cooking. They planned to cook two whole goats, twelve chickens, a huge pot of soup, and to bake fifty pies and cakes. Boxes and boxes of wine were carried into the house. Master Moron was expecting more than 100 guests.

Mefrou, who appeared in a becoming light yellow dress, was made comfortable on a chaise lounge, where she could enjoy the party from a reclining position.

The biggest surprise of the day was when a carriage pulled by four beautiful horses arrived at the plantation and Master Chris stepped out.

Mai Sila and Didi ran out of the kitchen, leaving all the work behind, when Mimina came to tell them about the surprise. Mai Sila grabbed a plate of sweets and Didi a plate with egg rolls. Any excuse was good enough to see "Baby Chris." Neither of the women could believe their eyes when they saw him. He was tall and handsome and dressed for a salon party. His face was still long and white, but more mature, and his hair was still spikey and pale blond. To Didi and Sila, he looked like the most handsome man in the whole room.

Didi stood, back to the wall, to observe her "son" as he spoke with a friend of Miriam's who was making eyes at him. She felt like screaming to him, "She is not worth it! It is because you studied in Europe and your father is Master Moron that she looks at you. She is just concerned with your estate." But Didi knew better than that. She wished she could hug him and ruffle his hair as she used to do when they were young. Hungrily her eyes followed him, taking in all his features.

When he turned around and saw her, a broad smile lit up his face. He left the girl and walked straight to where Didi was standing.

"Mai Didi, Mai Didi," he kept repeating. Then he gave her a big bear hug, right there in the party room, for all to see. "Mai Didi, how I missed you," he said laughing.

Didi tried to push him away. "Master Chris, people are looking; it is not appropriate."

He gave her a quick peck on her cheek and said with a wink, "I imagine they will look. But I don't care. See you later, Mai Didi." Master Moron politely ushered his son away from Didi and into the company of the party guests.

Didi sleepwalked back to the kitchen where she and Mai Sila could not stop talking about Master Chris.

"Didi, he didn't forget you, he came right up and hugged you!" Sila exclaimed. "And that in a room full of people!"

Chapter Nineteen

Chris was not the only one who received a lot of attention that night. Miriam, princess-like in her stunning new dress, met Mijnheer Waterman, the brother of one of her friends. Mijnheer Waterman chose to dance with her many times and looked deeply into her eyes when they talked. Miriam was glowing. Nothing could be more perfect than her 15th birthday party.

After the party, Miriam called Mimina out to the porch to talk with Chris. Mimina declined because she saw how much cleaning up had to be done after the party. All the slaves were exhausted, and the next day their work was waiting for them just like always.

Miriam insisted and ordered Mai Sila to send Mimina to join her and her brother. The reason for this desperate plea soon became clear. The queen of the ball needed someone to listen to her repeating time after time how Mijnheer Waterman had invited her for dinner. She needed Mimina to help her plan. What would she wear? How would she look? What should she say? How would she approach him? She kept dreaming.

Chris smiled at his sister's naïve chatter. Chris and Mimina immediately hit it off again, as though the years that he was absent had melted away.

If anyone would have seen the three of them sitting on that porch, eating leftovers and chatting, they would not have known that these were two masters and a slave girl. Social relationships were not important at this moment. For that one night, there were no color barriers, no racial differences, no master-slave positions—just friendship. They felt like kids again. Mimina was drunk with happiness. She had missed her friendship with Miriam so much.

It was not until Didi came back and called her to continue working that she reluctantly left her friends on the porch.

***

Chris stayed on at the plantation to be with his mother. He spent all his time in her room or carried her to the garden or to the porch so they could be together. She blossomed under his attention and love. He shared with her all he learned in the Netherlands and answered her questions about her family over-seas.

Didi spoke seriously with Mimina about spending time with Chris. "I don't want you hanging around with Master Chris all the time. He is a man now and I have seen his eyes looking at you."

"But Mai, that is not possible. Chris is like my brother," Mimina said.

Didi didn't give up. "Child, when there is a slave involved, there is no brotherhood. He could send for you anytime and demand submission." Her voice was trembling. "And a white man is never a brother of a black. Not even in church."

"I am sorry Mai, I didn't think about Chris in that way. I trust him. He wouldn't do that to me. We are friends."

Didi shook her head. "I don't want you in the house when he is here, Mimina, and that is my final word. I do not have a good feeling about this."

Mimina's mouth hung open. Her mother had never put her foot down so firmly about anything.

"And I cannot send you to Punda. There are so many bad men in Punda. I am not sure how I am going to keep you out of the Big House..." Didi shook her head and looked miserable.

Mimina let out a big sigh. Didi had been to Punda a total of two times in her life, but she "knew" about bad men in Punda. Mimina knew there was no arguing with her mother. She took a deep breath and gave in. "I will stay in our room and send a message that I am not feeling well. I know Chris will be leaving for Punda soon."

With her head down, Mimina walked to her dark old room. How could she stay there for days? She planned to get up very early in the morning and make some candles and oils, so she would have something to do.

Didi walked straight to her *Mefrou* and told her that Mimina was coming down with something and would be staying in her room.

Mefrou was surprised to hear this, as Mai Yeye, Sila, and Didi had never allowed sickness to keep them from their work before. She studied Didi's agitated face and flinching eyes. "That is okay, Didi. I don't want people to become sick, especially with Master Chris in the house. Mimina is a beautiful child and we should protect her." She understood the situation.

Didi managed to keep Mimina out of sight for more than a week. Finally the day arrived when she could not come up with more excuses. She assigned Mimina to work in the detached kitchen and warned her not to wander into or close to the Big House.

"If anything happens to you, scream and run. I should have run. My master would have helped me, but I didn't know it then. Master Moron or *Mefrou* will certainly help you."

Miriam sent Didi to fetch Mimina as soon as she heard Mimina was working again. They spent their time in Miriam's room planning the outing. Mimina did not see Chris and she missed him, but to prevent something bad happening, she purposely avoided him.

One evening Miriam asked for Mimina while Chris was with her in her room. "Mimina, come do my hair for me," she summoned Mimina.

Chris was sitting on the chair opposite them and Mimina felt his eyes on her.

"I want to do my hair with pearls for my date and I want you to start practicing now. Just weave the pearls through my hair before you braid it and see how it looks." And to Chris she said, "Please Chris, don't leave. I want your opinion too."

Mimina was uncomfortable but she could not ignore the request. The whole time she worked, she felt Chris's eyes on her back. When their eyes met, she looked quickly away. "It looks like Mai Didi was right," she thought, and made a firm decision not to be alone with Chris again.

Miriam kept sending for Mimina as she planned and schemed about her upcoming date with Mijnheer Waterman. The seamstress was summoned to the plantation. Miriam and *Mefrou* spent hours talking with her and going through fabrics to choose the right one. Mimina was fanning them and was able to observe all the possibilities.

Since Miriam had not been endowed with a full figure, most of the talk was to determine how the dress would need to be cut to make it look like she had more of a bosom. Stella, the seamstress, was to sew a dress that was wider at the top so it could be filled with cotton balls.

Miriam chose a heavy material elaborately decorated with gold stripes, but Stella advised her against that choice. "For a first dinner the young ladies usually choose a simple white or light yellow dress. We could make a long stole to enhance it a little, but no dark colors and no shiny material. That is more for older ladies," she said.

Mefrou agreed and Stella was put to work. She would bring four dresses the next week for fitting, all suitable for young ladies to go out on a date. The teacher was summoned so she could prepare to be the chaperone, due to the illness of *Mefrou*. All was set. Miriam was excited.

Precisely during the week of the great event, *Mefrou's* sickness took a bad turn, and completely unexpectedly, she passed away. Master Moron, who had arrived from Punda with Le Docteur, took it badly. He was completely unprepared for the departure of his wife.

Le Docteur could only confirm that her death was due to natural causes.

Mefrou Wilhelmina was no more. The plantation was in deep mourning. Miriam and Chris were overtaken with grief.

Master Moron asked the medicine women to prepare the body. It was logical that they should do so, having lived so closely with *Mefrou*.

Master Moron walked around the plantation as though in a trance. He had never expected his wife to die and leave the children in his care. They were still young and not even married yet.

Miriam sent word to Mijnheer Waterman that their outing could not take place.

The slaves blew their horns for hours. Not much work was done that day. Fito tried to accomplish something, but even he was absentminded. Uncertainty hung in the air for the slaves. "Which one would be saved? Who would be sold?"

In the afternoon, the slaves came after work time to pay their respects. They stood with Fito in the yard and waited for their Master to come onto the balcony to talk to them. Some of them were inconsolable.

Master Moron and Chris stood in the porch and thanked the slaves for coming. The master said, "I want to thank you all for coming and suffering with us in this difficult time. I want you to know that the work will continue as always. Fito will be in charge, the same as when I am in Punda. There will be no changes, nobody will be sold or sent away. I want you to remain calm and help me now by working hard so we can get the corn in before the rains start."

A collective sigh of relief escaped from the slaves. No changes. That was good. The husbands hugged their crying wives and the mothers their sons. Everybody had been frantic since the news arrived.

Sitting on the porch drinking some port, Moron was in deep thought. Mai Sila brought him a plate of cold chicken. He looked up and saw that tears were still visible on her face. She really was hurting for her *Mefrou*. It was heartfelt.

It did Moron good to notice that his slaves really loved his wife. Maybe now was a good time to free them? With Wilhelmina gone, he could afford it. Maybe... maybe he should wait a little, let everything settle down. Tomorrow he was leaving for Punda with Chris, and Miriam would be alone.

***

Here's your passage with corrected punctuation and proper paragraphing, keeping every single word exactly as you wrote it:

***

Miriam cried, threw a tantrum—which used to work, but didn't now—to be allowed to go to Punda with her father and brother. Master Moron was firm.

"You are in mourning and you will stay home. I will have no daughter of mine going on social visits dressed in black. When your mourning period is over, you can join us in Punda. That was my last word, Miriam. You can go to your room now."

Miriam stood up from the dining table and threw her fork down.

"You don't love me! You take Chris and you leave me with some slaves here in this big, God-forsaken house."

She ran to the door.

"That is not true and you know it, Miriam. Chris is working. He will not be attending balls," Master Moron began. But his words were in vain. Miriam already had left the dining room. Master Moron gave Mimina a sign to follow his daughter and she obediently did as he asked.

Miriam was inconsolable. Continuing her tantrum like a small child, she hit the table, the wall, and the door. With soft words and soothing touch, Mimina managed to calm her down until Chris came. He was always able to soothe her.

Mimina cleaned the broken lamp, vases, and glasses which didn't survive the outburst. She was leaving the room when Miriam screamed again, demanding that Mimina stay with her. Mimina sat down and held her hands while Miriam cried softly. Mimina wiped her face and kept murmuring soft words until Miriam was calm again.

Chris and Mimina looked each other in the face. Neither said a word. They sat there until Miriam fell asleep.

Chris went to the porch and asked Mimina to sit with him. But she declined, claiming that she needed to help her mother prepare dinner.

"I had such high hopes that we would meet again and spend time together. But you are always working or in the woods. I never get to see you."

"Master Chris, we are not children anymore. I am the slave in this house. I need to care for you all. I cannot be sitting and talking. There is a flu going around in the huts. At least four children have died already. It might have been the same flu that *Mefrou* died from. We need to make medicine all the time. We need to care for Miriam, for the house, and for the meals. I cannot sit around."

"Why do you call me 'Master' Chris?" he asked. "You don't call Miriam 'Yufrou' Miriam; why the formality with me?"

Mimina groped for words. She could not explain.

"I...I really need to help Mai..." she murmured and ran to the kitchen.

The next morning Master Moron and Chris left for Punda. Peace returned to the house. The teacher arrived the same morning to be the live-in chaperone. Miriam was strongly against this, claiming she didn't need a babysitter. But Teacher kept a strong hand on her, which was more than *Mefrou* was ever able to do.

More and more, Miriam sent for Mimina, and Teacher could do nothing about that. As Miriam put it, "Mimina is MY personal slave. I NEED her to be here for me. My father gave me this slave when I was born and you cannot take her away from me."

Mimina tried to engage her in sewing, reading poems, doing water painting, or roaming the woods, but Miriam wanted only to talk about Mijnheer Waterman. She could talk about him all day long and invented scenarios so she could see him before her mourning was over. She made Teacher send a message to the parents of her friends, inviting them for a quiet tea "to cheer her up."

The girls arrived, properly dressed in dark colors and escorted by the older sister of one of them. Mimina served the tea and fanned the visitors afterward. Miriam was chatting in high spirits and the girls were sharing a lot of giggles. The big sister wandered off and sat on the porch, reading her book.

Mimina wished she could leave too. Miriam was so spoiled sometimes. She heard her gossiping about her other friends who were not present today. How could she? Mimina wished she had friends other than Miriam, who technically was her owner. Her arms were hurting. The fan started to feel heavier and heavier every minute. And it didn't look like the girls were paying attention.

She looked over the table. The sandwiches were gone. Could she go to the kitchen and make another snack so she could stop fanning? Would they mind? She glanced over to the girls, who were sitting with their heads close to one another, sharing something that made Miriam's face red.

Mimina judged this to be the exact good time to quietly leave the room. At the door she threw them a glance. Just as she thought, they didn't notice she was leaving.

She ran to the kitchen and got herself a cup of tea while quickly making some nice thin sandwiches with chicken salad, exactly as Miriam liked. She didn't take time to eat anything even though she still hasn't had a bite since breakfast.

She rushed back to the room and lowered the plate onto the table, hoping nobody had missed her. Then she took her fan up again and started waving it.

Miriam's head shot up and a shriek escaped her mouth.

"I don't believe you!" she screamed to her friend Suzanna, while wildly waving her hands in the air and almost hitting her.

"I am sorry I said that, Miriam; maybe it is not true." Suzanne was very apologetic.

"I spoke with Rosy yesterday at the book reading tea party at Miss Jones' house, and she told me she soon will be engaged to Mijnheer Waterman. She said the invitations for the engagement party were on their way," Jody chimed in.

"Yes, my mother said Mijnheer Waterman was very taken with Rosy and with her father's plantation. They own a huge plantation with over 80 slaves," Rebecca added.

Miriam's face turned red and she was obviously upset, although she did her best not to cry in front of her friends. The party was not so fun after this episode, and the friends said their quick good-byes.

It was as though Miriam's world had come crashing down. She cried and threw things for days. Mimina took all breakable items from her room. She sent a quiet message for Chris and he came late in the night to speak with his sister. The next morning he left again, leaving a sad but calmer Miriam.

Teacher took the dejected girl horseback riding and visiting some of Teacher's family members. They were gone for two days, but when they came back Miriam kept talking about Mijnheer Waterman. The difference was that now she could remember only his bad side. He was too short for her anyway; he was only interested in her father's possessions; and he was a mama's boy.

Soon Mimina was spending hours fanning Miriam and generally looking out for her welfare. Miriam didn't want to sleep alone anymore and made Mimina sleep in her room on a mat in the corner. In the night she would call Mimina and demand water, hot milk, or attention. Sometimes, this went on until the early morning.

When Mimina got up to start her early morning work, she was exhausted and could not function properly. After that went on for a week, Mimina developed headaches and dark circles under her eyes.

Mai Didi was concerned and made a strong tea, which she served to Miriam to make her sleep. Thus, sanity returned to the home.

Chapter Twenty

Master Moron, updated by Chris and Teacher, returned home to check on his daughter.

Miriam was elated when she heard the excited voice of one of the garden boys announcing the coming of the Master's carriage. She took Mimina with her and they stood at the gate to receive the men in her family. Master Moron and Chris were accompanied by Adam... and his family. Mimina smiled happy when she saw the family. She was an active member of the prayer group and one of their urgent prayers was for Adam to be reunited with his family.

Miriam hung on her father's neck. They walked into the Big House laughing and chatting, forgetting Mimina. She got a chance to give Adam a quick hug and to meet his wife, Ula, and their sons. The oldest son, Ruben, threw one glance at Mimina and was smitten. He had never seen such a beautiful girl before, he told his father later. With the golden sun beams on her skin, she glowed like bronze. Her body had developed into that of a young woman, and her hair lay in thick shining braids on her head, resembling a crown. Her young breasts stood out and her hands were long and well formed. Ruben could only imagine how the legs would be under her long skirts. Ruben was sold. Nobody else mattered.

That same week he asked Mimina to hold hands. But she was shocked and declined his offer.

"No, thank you," she said. "I am too young for these things. And I am very busy in the house. This is a difficult time for the family."

Ruben was determined. He even spoke to Didi. Both Didi and Mimina were livid about this. Didi was upset because she thought it impertinent of the boy to talk with her about those things without his father present. And Mimina was angry because now she was in trouble with Mai Didi about holding hands with boys, although she was completely innocent.

"Mimina, haven't you seen enough around you to know what is good and what is not? I want you to wait with holding hands. There is no hurry. You will find a husband soon enough."

Mimina didn't want to argue with her mother. She was not really interested in Ruben or any other person anyway. She had not figured out if she wanted to be married.

"Mai Didi, I don't really like this boy that way. He asked me to hold hands but I did tell him that I am not ready."

"You are only sixteen, just wait till you find somebody that loves God and that is made for you. Thank God, Master Moron let the house slaves choose their own partners. You are not forced to produce children to work in the field and break their backs doing it. So choose wisely. Wait on God."

"Mai Didi, every man around us is a slave. How am I going to find a man if he's not a slave? My children will end up in the field anyway."

"God will help you. You might find somebody that at least can buy his freedom eventually."

Mimina was quiet, but she was not convinced.

Ruben was not easily diverted. He persisted and kept asking Mimina out. He approached her again and asked her to go with a group to a neighborhood plantation the next day after dark. There would be a marriage party there and his father, Adam, was the preacher. She could go and enjoy a party.

A party!

Mimina was excited. She only knew the tea parties from *Mefrou* or Miriam in which she was always the servant and the one that fanned the guests. To be a guest? In a real party? In her whole life, she had never heard slaves had parties. But this was a special occasion, since the man who was getting married was the fito from the other plantation. Even if it would be a slave marriage, it was something

Mimina never had seen before, and she was excited about the possibility.

Didi wasn't so thrilled about the party. Adam came by during the day and invited Didi and Mai Sila to join them. A whole group of them would walk over and celebrate together with the fito from that plantation who was to be married by Adam. That was why both the Masters had given their consent.

So it was decided that the whole family would go.

Mimina was bubbling. She was going to a party! Imagine.

Mimina dreamed about the party for the whole day. What was she going to wear? She owned only two dresses, a coarse dress for everyday work and a finer cotton one for Sundays. Neither of them sounded good enough to wear to a real party.

She remembered with sadness her youthful days when she would receive all of Miriam's used clothes. But with her developed body, Miriam's clothes no longer fit her. If she had time, she could make a dress out of two of Miriam's old dresses. But the party was tomorrow.

Suddenly Mimina remembered Miriam's new dress—THE new dress, the one Miriam was going to wear to the dinner party with Mijnheer Waterman! It was a simple dress, light yellow with a very elegant stole over it. If she could borrow it, she would wear it without that stole. It would definitely be too much to wear such an elaborated stole at a slave's wedding. But the simple basic dress would work well.

The good thing was that the dressmaker had made a top wide enough for Miriam to stuff it with cotton and enhance her figure, so it would fit Mimina now. If only she could try the dress on, she would know if it would fit. Without a second thought and with that lovely light yellow dress in her mind, she walked quickly to find Miriam.

Miriam was not in her room. Mimina found her sitting on the porch talking with Chris and Master Moron. Mimina hid between the two huge white pillars. The big green fern was in front of it so she could sit there unwatched and wait for them to finish talking.

Patiently waiting, Mimina dreamed about the dress and the party. Mentally she was making adjustments. The conversation on the porch was not too interesting for her and she didn't follow it until she heard Master Moron saying, "I will be staying in Punda. I will take permanent residence there. I am investing heavily now in cocoa from South America and it is going well. Chris, you will take over the running of the plantation. Miriam, you will act as the hostess. The medicine women will stay here. And they will help you as they helped your mother."

Mimina was alert now and focused on the conversation on the porch. What were they saying about them?

Master Moron was still speaking. "Miriam, you will need to plan the menus, authorize the orders, count the deliveries, sign off on them and order cleaning and repairs. The medicine women were faithful to your mother. You can depend on them for the house to be organized, and it would be great training for you to run the house."

Miriam was whining. "I hate stuffy things like making menus and ordering things, Papa; you know that. I want to go to Punda with you and meet more people."

Chris said, "Papa, now that you mention the medicine women, I remember something important I wanted to ask you about them. Grandpa Pe asked me to remind you about the issue with the medicine women. He said you would know what I am talking about. He wanted you to settle it right away. Do you know what I am talking about?"

Mimina's mouth fell open. She had heard a lot about Master Pe and *Mefrou* Jo. Mai Sila was sad when they learned of Master Pe's death. But what could he have said to Master Moron? She stood as quietly as possible, trying to hear more while scanning the hallway for Mai Sila or Mai Didi. Both would scold her for sure if they found her eavesdropping. The dress and the upcoming party flew out of her mind. She dared to lean forward to see what was going on, on the porch. This was serious; this was big. But what was it? What was going on? She sensed the importance of it without understanding what was happening. She watched her Master's face. It was red and angry... or maybe not angry, but uncomfortable? What could Master Pe have said to make Master Moron react like that? Mimina strained to hear more.

Master Moron was shaking his head while he said, "Yes, I know what Grandfather was referring to."

Chris, expecting an explanation, said, "So? What was it? What did Grandfather want you to do for the medicine women?"

That was exactly what Mimina wanted to know!

But Master Moron was not going to tell them. She watched while he looked uncomfortable and then obviously made up an answer.

"He just asked me to take good care of them since they have been so faithful to our family. Don't worry, son, I am aware of his wishes."

Chris was not convinced. "But... but... father, I am sure Grandpa was talking about something more. He said he wrote you about it but you never replied. He was talking about it on his deathbed. It had to do with Master Jan and the slave papers."

Mimina was anxious to know too. Her heart was beating fast. Master Jan. That was her grandfather. She felt that the answer to that question would change her life. Mentally she went through the Master's desk. Where would he keep an important letter from Master Pe? She thanked God that she could read. If she found that letter, she could read it to her mother and grandmother. But, of course, they would never allow her to read a letter from the Master.

Master Moron was still ruminating, trying to come up with a good answer for his son.

"Chris, I have always treated the medicine women with respect and plenty of food. They are well cared for. You do not need to worry about them. You just came back from Europe, and you don't know the dynamics of being responsible for many people. Especially the slaves. They are like children. We need to care for them. They would never survive on their own. Do you know how difficult it is for some women to survive on their own without a man to take care of them? Our slaves have a good life here on the plantation. They don't need anything else. It will be your task to take good care of each one of them now so they can work and produce. That is how it works." Master Moron's voice was definitive.

Mimina watched Chris's face closely and saw that he was not convinced, and neither was she. Master Moron had 60 good slaves. Why would Master Pe send a message from Europe after all those years to take good care of some women slaves? It didn't make sense to her nor, obviously, to Chris.

Miriam didn't care. She drank her tea and looked dreamingly over the gardens.

Chris nodded to his father and walked away so fast that Mimina could not get away in time. She pressed herself closer to the pillar behind the fern leaves and held her breath. Thankfully, he barged past without noticing her. Quickly she followed and didn't stay to wait for Miriam. She went to the kitchen to tell her family what she overheard.

The news left them flabbergasted. Master Pe wrote about them? Mai Sila never forgot those Masters, and once more she told the story about their love. "If Master Pe wrote anything, it could only be something that was good for us." She was convinced.

That same evening, Master Moron sent for the medicine women and the Fito to come to his office. A scared and agitated Sila came to fetch them.

"Please do not panic," Master Moron said. "I just want to tell you about some of the changes I am going to make on the plantation. I will be living permanently in Punda and I will hand this plantation over to Chris. He will be in charge and manage it. The teacher will live here with Miriam until she gets married. She needs to learn to manage this house by herself. I will need your help, Didi and Mimina, for the home affairs."

Turning to Fito he said, "My residence and business in Punda is growing so fast that I need a reliable Fito for my townhouse. I have decided to take you with me tomorrow when I leave. Sila will be coming too, so you will be together. Adam will be the new Fito working with Chris..."

His voice trailed off when he saw the impact his words were having on his slaves.

Mai Sila swooned, her legs weakening, and the Fito reached for her. Mimina and Didi were on her side and held her. All three of them were crying. Mai Sila was trembling violently. Punda was the worst place in the world for her. She had been there one more time after she came to live on this plantation so many years ago after Didi was born. She remembered Master Jan in Punda.

Master Moron moved around impatiently. Crying women were clearly not his thing. "I really need you Sila," he said soothingly. "I have sent for *Mefrou* Jo, she will be arriving soon from Holland and I need a medicine woman to take care of her. She is not so healthy. She forgets things and need constant care, I hear. She knows you and you liked her, so I need you in Punda. And I have now almost ten slaves living in the townhouse, they need care too. Please don't cry. You can come to the plantation with Adam to greet your family and they can come to Punda too."

The family sat outside under the tamarind tree that night and talked long hours about Mai Sila's move with the Master, and more importantly the news Mimina brought about a letter. Could it possibly mean that Master Pe was asking for their freedom? None of them dared to dream that big. Maybe Mai Sila could discover more from *Mefrou* Jo once she arrived on the boat.

The party broke up when Didi went to the Big House to check on her masters, Sila and Fito went to pack and say goodbye to their friends, and Mimina went to check on Miriam's needs. In Miriam's room, she prepared the bed and opened a window to let the cool breeze come into the room. If the room was too hot, Miriam would ring for her and she would be fanning Miriam until she slept. To keep busy she swept the floor and waited for Miriam to come.

This looked like a good time to ask Miriam for her dress. She was excited again, dreaming about her big outing. She was sure Miriam would help her dream and share her happiness. Hadn't she, Mimina, lived all of Miriam's dreams with her when Mijnheer Waterman was still in the picture?

As soon as Miriam arrived in the room Mimina said, "I have great news. Ruben, Adam's son, has asked me to go to a party with him. It is the fito of Plantation West that is getting married and the masters have given permission for a celebration. Ruben wants to hold hands with me....!" The excited Mimina was rolling over her words to get them out as quickly as possible to her friend.

Miriam didn't react at first as expected.

"Who is Ruben?" she asked, in a less-than-excited voice.

Mimina explained it to her again. "Don't you remember the new boy that came to live on the plantation with his father, Adam?"

"Oh... a son of Adam? But he is a slave. Why would you want to hold hands with a slave?" asked Miriam while she analyzed her nails.

Chapter Twenty One

Mimina was once more astonished by the insensitivity Miriam displayed. That was the thing she could not fathom about her friend. Miriam could be so inconsiderate. Mimina wished she could ask Miriam with whom she was supposed to go out, since she was a slave. But Mai Didi's instructions about proper behavior for a slave were burned into her mind, and she didn't lose patience with her mistress. She just shrugged.

"I heard Mijnheer Waterman had already bought the engagement ring for 'stupid Rosy,' " Miriam said, going back to her favorite topic.

Mimina held her breath. Please God, do not let Miriam get started about Mijnheer Waterman now. Quickly she said, "Ruben is the one who helped you get onto the horse last week when you went riding with Teacher. He has big black afro hair. Remember him?"

"I remember him; he was a stable hand. He did look cute indeed, for a slave," Miriam said absent-mindedly.

This gave Mimina more hope to ask. "I want to ask you if I could try out your yellow dress. The new one with a bigger cup. I would like to look nice at the party and I don't have any dresses..."

Before Mimina finished talking, she noticed that something went wrong. Miriam's face was twisted and became very red. When she opened her mouth, a string of curses flew out.

"Are you crazy, Mimina! You are a slave, you cannot even think about wearing one of my dresses. And certainly not to go holding hands with an ugly, black slave nikker that works in the fields, for heaven's sake." Without warning, she hit Mimina in the face.

Mimina was shocked and took a step backwards, tripping over the bed and falling. She hit her head and tears began to stream from her eyes.

Miriam, completely out of control, grabbed her by the hair and pulled her up.

"Slave, be quiet!" she ordered, and gave Mimina another blow. "Shut up! You are disrespecting orders. I will punish you for that."

Miriam had seen many times how her friends treated their slaves, and she used it all. She grabbed a belt and hit Mimina over and over again. The belt lashed Mimina's face, back, arms, and whole body. Miriam just kept hitting all the spots she could find to hit while she was screaming, "Ugly black nikker, who do you think you are? Do you think you can go out on a Saturday night while I stay home waiting for a suitable husband? And on top of that, you want to wear my dress? The dress that I was going to wear for Mijnheer Waterman? But no, he goes out and buys a ring... a ring... for that stupid Rosy and you... want to wear my dress to go with a nikker!"

Mimina couldn't take it anymore. She was screaming. It seemed that the harder she screamed, the harder and more carelessly Miriam hit her.

Just then, the door to the room flew open and Chris stormed in. "Miriam! What are you doing?" he shrieked, and dove forward to detain her when she prepared to strike again.

Miriam turned on him with the belt while screaming, "This slave is impudent. She does not show respect and should be punished. She is mine! My father gave her to me so I can do with her whatever I want."

Her face was twisted in an angry, ugly mask. Nothing in her looked like the young girl she was. Out of her mouth came a string of profanity which Chris didn't even know she knew. It was as though a dam broke and a stream of ugly, dirty water washed over them.

Chris wrestled her for the belt, saying, "Are you mad, Miriam? You cannot talk like that. This is Mimina, your friend."

"Mad? Mad? I will show you what mad is," Miriam screamed, and with a new lunge forward she freed herself from him and managed to kick Mimina in her stomach. "This nikker is not my friend. I hate her. She walks around with her big tits trying to be attractive. But she is a slave and she should know her place."

"Miriam, stop it right now! Mimina might be a slave by birth but she is also your friend. Her mother gave you milk at her breast for heaven's sake! You would have died if not for that slave woman. She took care of you your whole life. Why would you want to hurt Mimina now?" Chris tried to reason with her, but he was not getting through.

"Ha! Do you think I don't know why you are talking like that? You like her, don't you? I have seen your eyes watching her! But you cannot have her! She is a nikker. And my slave. I will never free her. You cannot marry a slave."

Her words hit Chris hard, but he didn't flinch. "You are out of control, young lady, and you are going to be calm right now and be still. I do not wish to hear anything anymore. I am your big brother and I am telling you what to do. You are my sister and I love you. You need to calm down."

He held tight to her and kept talking to her until he finally was able to quiet her.

Didi knocked and came in with a concerned look on her face. She too had heard the yelling and came upstairs as fast as her legs could carry her.

Chris gave her a sign to take Mimina out of the room. When Didi saw her lying on the floor, looking like she was dead, she fell to her knees in front of her. Moved to tears, she half dragged Mimina out of the room.

Chris stayed with his sister for the whole night.

Life changed drastically for the medicine women. Mimina's face was badly bruised and swollen. She hid in her room. There was no way she could go to any party like that. All she could do was cry.

It was as though someone very important to her had died. She cried for the beating, for the loss of her friend Miriam, for the party she could not go to, and for the pain. Her arms and back were black and blue. She barely could move.

For the first time in her life, she really understood what it meant to be a slave. Anyone who owns her could beat her up, sell her, send her to work in Punda or to come back and work on a plantation, violate her, or worse.

She was just a slave. The desolate feelings that attacked Mimina's heart were indescribable. She could not completely understand what was happening with her. Mimina grew up in one night.

Didi was there with her, making her cold compresses, but nothing could lessen Mimina's grief.

Mimina stayed in bed for two days. The day she went back to work Miriam became Yùfrou Miriam to her. As much as possible, Didi gave Ruby the task of serving Miriam at the table.

Now that Mai Sila had left for Punda, Didi was in charge of the kitchen and Ruby's sister, Kela, came to help in the house. Mimina helped her mother in the kitchen and took charge of almost all the preparation of the medicines. With that came the big responsibility of visiting sick slaves and treating them. She was kept busy and did not often serve in the house anymore.

One morning Master Chris sent for Mimina. With sad eyes he observed the rainbow of colors on Mimina's face and arms where his sister had beaten her. He apologized profusely for Miriam's behavior.

Mimina stood before him with her head down, her hands folded in front of her, in the perfect slave position. She risked a glance at him when she felt he was looking away. She could feel his desire for her. He was watching her intently. His eyes bright with... need?

At that moment, a devious plan began to grow inside Mimina's mind. She had found her revenge. She had found a way to pay them back. Courteously, she nodded to her Master, accepted his apologies, and left the room. She felt better than she had felt for a whole week. Excitement was bubbling inside her once again. She had a plan. She would pay back. She would hit hard. She would not be a receiver of the abuse of her masters like her mother and grandmothers were. She would take matters into her own hands.

Didi noticed something was going on with Mimina but her daughter didn't confide in her. Couldn't confide. Didi would never agree. While she was beating the white laundry clean, with the water splashing all over her, she kept murmuring, "Wait and see what I am gonna do to your family. Just wait and see. You called me 'dirty nikker'... how dare you... I am the one... that keeps you and your house clean... the one that cares for you... dirty nikker... you will find out how dirty I can play... soon."

That same night, when the Big House quieted down, Mimina walked to Master Chris's room. He was already in bed, reading a thick book. The oil lamp next to his bed gave enough light for him to see her clearly.

"Mimina!" he said, surprised, when she knocked and came in. "What are you doing here? Is everything all right? Miriam?"

"Everything is all right. I thought you might want company?"

Now that the moment of revenge was at hand, Mimina felt self-conscious. How would she do this? Her mother would be livid when she heard of it. But Mimina silenced her conscience and plunged forward, following the script she had prepared. "I could stay with you if you wish," she said, smiling.

Master Chris's eyes were as big as saucers, but he didn't deny what was offered him. He took with both hands such a generous proposition. When he noticed that Mimina was untouched, he closed his eyes and almost drew back; but his desire was stronger than his will, and he gave in to her.

Mimina didn't feel anything. Her revenge was too great. "I might be a nikker but your brother wants me." She kept repeating to herself. "He wants me, he wants me."

Later that night she went back to her room satisfied with her first step toward full humiliation of the Master's family.

****

Mimina couldn't believe her new place in life. She had always been a slave, of course, but she never FELT like a slave. It was just part of how life was. Now, for the first time, it was clear to her how much of a slave she was. She realized that she was nothing special. She was just another slave.

If she ever had counted herself special because of her nicer clothes or her special place in the household as a private slave to the owner's spoiled daughter, now she knew she had been wrong. She was just another slave. Miriam owned her and she hated Mimina.

Mimina went around feeling dead inside. She laughed mechanically and worked like a robot.

A sad Didi made their 'special tea' for Mimina to prevent her becoming pregnant. But Mimina, knowing full well what Didi was doing, poured the tea out. She WANTED to be pregnant. She wanted Chris to have a slave son so they could feel how humiliating it was.

She did all she could to be pregnant. "Mai Didi," she said on one of these occasions to her mother, "I am planning to be a free black woman someday. This Master will have to set his children free. This is our only chance to be free."

"Slavery is for none of us, my child. We are not slaves. We were free people in Africa. Somebody stole us and sold us and called us slaves. We have been praying for deliverance from it for generations. And I am convinced God will do it for us. You cannot do it by yourself. Remember what Mai Yeye used to tell us about Tula? They tried. Strong men in the prime of their lives. They tried but the evil succeeded. We need Jesus to save us. He is the only one bigger than the evil. Trust Him, child."

Mimina's trust in the Lord was long gone, probably with the first contact of the belt over her face or with the first humiliating words. She was not going to sit around and wait for an unseen God to intervene. And that was exactly what she told her mother.

"I was the same at your age, Mimina. And how I regret it. I will pray for you," Didi said.

As often as possible, Mimina went to the room of her Master. "If I have a son, he will know how it is to be a slave. His own son will be a slave. That will serve him right. Miriam's first nephew will be a slave. They can put their own family to work for them. And I know Chris. To avoid having a slave child he will need to set the child free and me also. Chris would never let his son grow up as a slave; he is too soft-hearted," she kept thinking.

In the spring of 1837 Mimina's hope was fulfilled. She became pregnant and her first son was born. Mai Sila arrived from Punda in time to help with the delivery. Didi was also there to help.

The precious little boy was born white, strong, and perfect. Mimina chose a white man's name for him. "He will need a strong name when he is free, Mother," she explained.

But her choice was not well received by her family. "I will call him Robertus Petrus. Petrus was the official name of Master Pe, so I actually named him after his grandpa!"

Master Chris was dumbfounded to be a father. And a father to a slave child. He never had foreseen this complication. He couldn't sleep at night.

He didn't know how to act. Should he give his son's mother special treatment? When was he going to see his son? How should he treat his son?

He was ill, slept poorly, and became thin. His sister fought with him, continually throwing his wrongdoings in his face.

When she sent word to her father about what was going on, Master Moron rushed to the plantation. He spent a night in the library with Chris and they screamed at each other.

Miriam sent for Mimina and accused her of "stealing her brother from her." She took the belt to Mimina once more.

As soon as Chris left, she began demanding services from Mimina every day and used the belt or the switch freely if her commands were not immediately obeyed.

There was nothing left of their friendship or sisterhood. Miriam was the mistress. A bitter mistress.

****

Nobody else asked for Miriam's hand in marriage. She was too thin, too bony, and had not enough curves for the current taste. She had nothing to offer other than a sour disposition. Besides, the gentlemen were not very interested, especially since Chris came back from Europe and took charge of the plantation.

Miriam tried her best to attract a man. She had Stella the seamstress over often to sew her the most elaborate dresses of the finest material they could find. The dresses were cut lower and lower to reveal more and more, but the sad part was that there was nothing to reveal.

Teacher stayed to chaperone her to the many parties she attended, hoping to find a husband. Sometimes Teacher would take her to Punda and they would spend months there.

Still no husband.

Chapter Twenty Two

Master Moron arranged to take Master Chris to Punda, where he stayed for six months. When he came back to the plantation, he was a married man. His wife was *Mefrou* Amy. It was a big surprise for all the slaves, but Miriam was smug in her victory. She had helped her father find a good wife for Chris.

The medicine women, with Ruby and Kela, were called to the library where Miriam introduced *Mefrou* Amy to them. She was a slender woman with long, shining black hair. Her big black eyes were skittish. She didn't look the slaves in the face but kept her own face lowered as if she were shy. Her voice was soft and very low. In the first weeks, the medicine women learned to strain to hear their *Mefrou* and follow up with her orders.

She gave an order in such a way that it sounded like a question. She would thank the staff profusely for whatever small thing they did for her. She was clearly not used to having slaves around to wait on her and she was a very easy *Mefrou* to please. She gave Didi carte blanche in the kitchen to produce whatever meal she wanted. She didn't say much. At the dinner table, she would talk with a soft voice to Miriam, but the two of them never became friends. She stayed pretty much in her private rooms. She loved embroidery and made perfect pieces that she placed around the house.

She didn't throw tea parties or visit any of the other plantations in the area. She was a quiet lady in her own room. The slaves almost didn't know she was there.

It had not been easy for Master Moron to find Chris a wife. He was just not interested in other girls. But Master Moron was adamant. His son could not live like that, having relations with a black woman, producing slave kids. He wanted better for his son. Silently, he gave thanks that the news of the slave baby had not reached Punda. Miriam was the only one that knew about it, and she was not going to disgrace herself by telling her friends that her brother preferred a black woman over a white one.

Master Moron had continued looking and didn't rest until he had found a wife for Chris. To make matters worse, Chris was not the handsomest young man. His long bony face lacked the grace that his mother had. He was interested in literature and history, not in being an elegant city boy walking around with his umbrella and high hat to find himself a dashing girl. Chris didn't like dancing or the balls his father arranged for him to attend. He talked with the young ladies one time and never followed up, leaving a trail of broken hearts.

Finally, Master Moron took matters into his own hands and arranged a marriage with Amy's father, who was having the same problem with his girl. She didn't want to go out to find a husband.

Mimina was shocked by what she called Chris's betrayal. Instead of freeing her and her slave son, he went to Punda and came back married to a nobody! Right away she decided to double her efforts. That same night she went to Master Chris's room and offered herself, pushing the right buttons she had learned in the previous months. He tried hard to convince her he was a married man now and could not betray his wife.

It didn't work. Mimina was not going to be convinced and Chris fell for the temptation. After that first night, they established a new routine. Mimina would come and offer herself and he would receive her, not able to withstand her wiles.

In 1839 Jacques Sebastian was born, another beautiful baby boy. He was followed, three years later in 1841, by Ronaldus Willem. Mimina was satisfied. She had three sons by her Master. Three healthy, strong sons. And the Master had none by his wife. Of course, he had none by his wife because Mimina took care of *Mefrou*'s tea every morning. And she made sure the tea was strong! She was determined. Her Master would only have slave sons. Until he freed them, that is.

Under continued strain, Master Chris decided to take his wife for a long trip to Europe. The plan was to visit some family and find a doctor to see why *Mefrou* was not getting pregnant. A gloomy Mimina saw them off. There was nothing she could do now. Life was easy on the plantation since the family was gone. Master Moron came back periodically to check on things, but everything was under control with Adam as Fito.

It took much longer than everybody expected for Master Chris and his wife to come back from their trip. Almost a year after they departed, they arrived all smiling and happy. *Mefrou* Amy was expecting.

They stayed for one week on the plantation and then went back for Punda. *Mefrou* Amy was not feeling well and she wanted to stay with her mother until the baby came. The slaves never saw her again.

Master Chris came alone when he came to supervise the plantation. Mimina would make sure she came to his bed at night. Usually, it was to persuade her Master to act on behalf of her sons. On this particular night she was seeking a better education for her sons.

"Teacher is in the house and she doesn't have anything to do," she said while caressing his hair. "Why not let her use some time in the morning and teach my sons reading and writing? I would like them to be educated."

Master Chris agreed easily and, against Teacher's and Miriam's wishes, Mimina's children began classes. Chris had to stay longer on the plantation to make sure that Teacher and Miriam followed his orders. He used the time to take his sister to social events, hoping to find her a husband. She was still a tall and bony, almost scrawny, young woman. She loved to dress up in her revealing, shiny dresses and accompany her brother.

When he left for Punda she went with him to be there for the party season and try once more to meet an eligible young man. But once again she could not attend any parties that year. *Mefrou* Amy died in childbirth, taking a tiny baby girl with her. Master Chris was alone, broken, childless and under heavy strain. He knew his sins were catching up to him.

But a surprise was around the bend: quite unexpectedly, Miriam met Mijnheer Frederic. She had already given up all hopes of marriage. Mijnheer Frederick was a cousin of *Mefrou* Amy who regularly came from Europe to spend some time on the island. He was a professor at the University of Amsterdam and he was a widower.

After a suitable time for mourning, the plantation was once more in upheaval. Master Moron ordered the place painted and extensive maintenance done. He wanted a cleaning team to clean and prepare all the rooms for a huge party. Most of the slaves remembered the party for the coming of age of Miriam. But this party was, if possible, bigger and better. No costs were spared. The best of the best was bought and prepared. Master Moron brought a whole kitchen team from Punda, who took care of most of the baking and cooking.

The invitations were sent months in advance and the names on the guest list were impressive. Mijnheer Frederic was very well connected and many of his large family were in attendance. Stella was summoned to make Miriam a whole new wardrobe suitable for the cold weather in the Netherlands.

The Domi, the protestant pastor from the impressive Protestant church in the palace in Punda, came out to the plantation to marry the couple. Miriam summoned Mimina continually to help her with dressing, packing and preparing. Miriam wanted to take Mimina with her to the Netherlands but Mijnheer Frederic was strict about it.

"I understand you have had slaves your whole life, Miriam, but you will need to learn to live with hired help. I don't condone slavery."

Fortunately, Mimina was not subjected again to the rod, but they had a strict *Mefrou*-slave relationship. Just a couple of days after the official marriage, the couple sailed for their new home in the Netherlands.

As soon as Miriam left, Mimina made sure she was the new woman in charge of the house. She didn't bother going to her own room at night anymore. She stayed with her Master the whole night. She stopped all pretexts and it was out in the open: Mimina lived with the Master. With the influence she had over her Master, she brought her three children out of their small, dark room into the Big House.

Master Chris gave permission to redo the big room in the attic next to the classroom. Their room was a big, airy one, and the boys had real beds with feather mattresses, not mats on the floor. They each had their own small closet and a table for doing their homework.

Mimina was proud when she looked back at what she had accomplished. She was settled in at the Big House, her children lived with her and there was no *Mefrou* or mean Master over them. With all her charms—her eyes, lashes, laughs and night visits—she had enticed her Master to do exactly what she wished. Yes, she had come a long way, but she was still a slave. How she coveted that piece of paper that said: FREE!

****

The Domi who performed Miriam's wedding came back a week later to talk with Chris. Mimina served them on the porch and left to help her mother prepare dinner for the guest. And once again she didn't hear the conversation that would change her life.

"Chris," said the Domi amicably, "I was happy last week to meet you. I know your father, of course. He is a faithful member of our congregation, but I was surprised to hear that he had a son. I never see you in church."

Chris's color reddened immediately. "I...I..." he stuttered while collecting his thoughts. "I knew this moment would come once I saw you coming to visit me and I don't know how to answer you, Domi. I don't want to lie to you, but I cannot come to church and be a hypocrite. I'd rather stay away from God until I am worthy."

"Worthy?" asked the Domi. "You don't feel you are worthy? Can you tell me more about it?"

Chris was squirming in his chair. His hands were sweating and he wiped them off on his shirt. He looked very uncomfortable and didn't answer right away. But the Domi didn't give up. "I have heard a lot of bad things over the years, Chris; you cannot shock me. Tell me what the matter is."

"I am not good with God, Domi, and I don't believe God can be interested in me. I have committed many sins. My soul is black. On top of it, I am estranged from my father. He came out here for the wedding, but that was the first time in a long time. After the party, we had a big fight again and he left. I am not his son anymore, he said. You see? Why would I go to church and pretend to be a nice man?" He wiped his eyes.

The Domi asked him, "Is that pretty slave that served us involved in your sins?"

Chris jumped up. "How did you know? Are people talking about me? Has the news reached Punda?"

"Sit down, Chris. Nobody told me. I didn't even know about you until I came out here for the wedding celebration. I just happened to notice just now how you followed her with your eyes when she was serving the drinks. She is a beautiful lady for sure."

Chris lowered his head and said in a very small voice, "I wish I could marry her. She is in my heart. But she is a slave. And my father will not free her. I have asked. He is afraid that if he freed her I would marry her and disgrace myself with the elite. As if I care for the elite."

"So you live with her as man and wife? Or do you use her when you have a need?"

Chris was burning with righteous indignation. "She is almost the mistress of this house. I have three sons with her." Forgetting all decorum, he started crying uncontrollably. The words he had kept to himself for so long came rolling out.

"The only sons that I have are slaves. They need to call me Master. I cannot touch them, send them away to be educated or just spend time with them. They work for me! What have I done?"

Domi moved closer to him and put a hand on his back but didn't speak.

Chris kept talking. "My sons are handsome. They have the strong bone structure from their mother. Their color is like bronze. Their faces are strong. They are good workers. I try to give them a good life, good food. I have allowed them to live in the house. But in the meantime, I have never given them a hug in my whole life. Why should I have slave sons? Why should I love a black woman?"

Master Chris held his head in his hands and sobbed. He was doubled over, as though in pain.

Domi let him cry until the worst was over. It took a long time. "I am happy I came here today. I see that you need help. Chris, don't panic. There are many things you can do to remedy this situation. I am willing to help you think and plan. The first and most important thing you need to do is to make sure you are good with God again. Because it is from God you need to receive help when you are going to straighten out your life. You need to reconcile with God."

"How? How can I reconcile? Having fathered three illegitimate sons? Not being able to free them because they will leave me? Scared of what people would say?"

"The first thing you need to do, and you just did it, is to admit your wrongdoings. Admit to God that you are a sinner. And then we can work from there. You can ask God to forgive you and help you make amends."

Domi kept his eyes on Chris when he was speaking, making sure he was with him. "Would you like to be with God? Would you like to experience forgiveness for your sins? If so, I can pray with you and ask God to change you."

Master Chris was still. He listened to the words and a small ray of hope came into his heart. Could there be a way out of the mess he had made for himself? Could he possibly be restored by God? Forgiven?

Domi prayed with Chris and the two men stayed for hours in the library talking. Together they went to their knees and humbly presented Chris to God, asking God for forgiveness and a new beginning.

Chapter Twenty Three

That night Chris went to his bed without dinner. He called for Mimina, but Ruby told him Mimina was in the slave huts helping with a baby. He ordered Ruby to tell Mimina not to disturb him that night. He wanted to be alone. He was sick, and he didn't want food or any other service.

"Please don't let anyone disturb me tonight."

A wide-eyed Ruby ran to tell Mimina, who was very upset with the news. For years, she had not been denied access to his bedroom. That night Mimina slept with her sons. She hoped to see Master Chris in the morning.

But just after she brought the water into the kitchen at 5:00 A.M., a slave ran to tell her about an emergency in the huts. She hurried out to help a child with a broken leg, and by the time she came back and helped with the normal work in the house, it was late. It was coconut oil day, and Mai Didi was busy with that. Ruby and Mimina served the table for Master Chris, but Mimina didn't dare to speak privately with him in front of Ruby.

That night she went to Master Chris's room as usual and noticed that he was not there yet. She went to bed waiting for him and fell asleep. In the morning she was shocked to see that he had not come to bed. Something was really wrong. What was going on? Was Master Chris planning another wedding? Was he bored with her? Was that the reason Domi came to visit for so long?

Mimina was very worried and tried all day to come up with a reason to speak with him. But he didn't come to the dining table, and Mai Didi ended up bringing him a tray in his office. He told her to leave him alone. He was busy.

Later that day Mimina went back to the huts to check on the child's broken leg. When she came back, ready to talk with Master Chris if he wanted or not, she got the message that he had left for Punda and didn't know when he was coming back.

Master Chris stayed in Punda for three weeks. He sent no message to the medicine women. From Fito they heard that the Master had started going to church with the Domi. The news was astonishing. The last people to be concerned about God were the Master's family.

Mimina was convinced that Master Chris was preparing to be married again. She was livid and thought up all kinds of plans to deal with this situation. How she had hoped to have her children freed by now. They were growing rapidly, and still nothing had happened. If the Master came back with another woman, her children would need to live in the huts again, maybe work the fields. There was no way they could stay in the house and be kept busy with schooling and medicine preparations.

How were they going to survive that hard life as field slaves? She had trained them as medicine men, but the plantation hardly needed more medicine people. They would be valuable if sold to other plantations. Mimina was almost panicking. Should she wait till Master Chris came home with his new wife? Or should she take matters into her own hands and flee?

Mai Didi saw Mimina's turmoil. "My child, how many things don't we do like Mai Yeye told us? Don't we use her recipe for coconut oil? Don't we cook her chicken stew? Don't we use her pots and pans? Why wouldn't you believe the God she told us about her whole life?"

Mimina did not appreciate her mother's God-talks. "Mai, you know Ruben has taken over from Adam as a prayer leader. Since he became the new leader, I have not gone there again. Why would I go now?"

"Why wouldn't you, Mimina? Ruben is a nice man. He made his life with Pili and they have five children. He is not going to hold it against you that when he was 15 years old he wanted to hold hands with you, but you refused. You made your life and you have three children. Grow up." Didi's voice was stern, but Mimina looked doubtful.

Didi continued. "And Ruben can read the Bible in Spanish now. He taught himself to read. He is a smart boy." Mai Didi was obviously proud of Ruben.

Mimina knew that it was not Ruben who kept her from the prayer meetings. She was just not willing to trust a God that made her a slave, a God that didn't come through for her. The bitterness which started when she was fifteen years old grew and now controlled her heart. She was in no way the nice girl she used to be. Being a slave made her a monster, ready to strike anyone who was in her way on the path to freedom.

****

Mimina decided to increase the instruction hours for her children. After Teacher dismissed them from the classroom, their mother took them to the woods and tested their knowledge of plants. She made them prepare medicines and looked over their shoulders, correcting them where necessary. She showed them how to make soap, oil, and ointments. She stood next to them checking their progress and making them do it again and again until they got it right. How she wanted to take her boys to help her with a delivery, but that would be crossing a line for sure. Other than the actual birth procedure, she taught them all they needed to know to be prepared for a baby's arrival.

After three weeks, Master Chris came back to the plantation. He called Mimina into his library right away and said to her, "Mimina, I have something important to tell you." He didn't look her in the eyes but kept his face down. Mimina's heart was racing. She was sure he was going to be married. But to her surprise he said, "I realize that I have sinned against you and against God." His voice was shaking.

What was going on here? Was the Master turning religious on them? Or was it a scam, a smoke screen? Mimina watched him intently while he struggled to find the right words. She didn't say a word. She couldn't have anyway. She was so angry, she couldn't speak.

"Mimina, I have gotten myself into big trouble. I talked with the Domi and he is helping me to straighten out my life. The first thing I need to do is to break with sin in my life. I will not sleep with you anymore. It is not fair to you."

The hard words were out. Master Chris glanced over at Mimina. She stood in the perfect slave position, like a statue. When he looked her in the eyes, he saw that she was smoking mad. She lowered her eyes quickly, avoiding his.

"Say something, Mimina," Chris said.

"As you wish, Master, I will not be coming to your room anymore." Mimina took two steps backward and with a small nod, she left the room.

Rage surged through her. She went to the room she shared so long with her mother and screamed, frustrated. She cried the whole day. She wasn't sad, she was mad! She was sure the Master had pulled a trick on her.

Didi was distressed. She prayed the whole day under her breath for her daughter.

"Lord, shine your grace on Mimina. Forgive her, Father. It is all my fault. I raised her with too big ideas. She has lived in two worlds since she was young. I shouldn't have let her go to school. I didn't show her enough that she was a slave. Now my poor child wants to be a Master. But that is not gonna happen. She is a slave. For always, Father, help my child understand. Help her forgive and forget."

Mimina continued to be angry and thought of scenario after scenario of malicious ways to get revenge on her Master. But the truth was that she was helpless. She was a slave and there was no future for her or her sons ...

On Sunday morning, Master Chris asked Fito to assemble all the slaves in the backyard of the Big House. He went out and walked through the rows of men. When they were all gathered, he told them that, as of the next week, all children under the 15 years would be allowed to have one hour reading and writing classes on a daily basis. He had engaged a tutor from Punda who would teach Mimina's children in the morning and all the slave children in the afternoon. They would get an hour break from their work to attend class.

After his words sank in, the stunned slaves began to express themselves in a variety of ways. Some were crying, others were asking questions. Others voiced their opinion. Another surprise followed as the Master ordered Mai Didi to bring out the sandwiches he had her prepare and began to hand them out himself.

Some of the slaves didn't dare accept them and kept wiping their hands on their clothes. Master Chris coached them to come closer. Fito walked through the crowd and kept them calm. After that very strange Sunday morning, the members of the prayer group rushed back to their meeting place to give thanks to the Lord.

That was not the only change the plantation residents dealt with that week. Monday morning, before the horn sounded to wake the slaves and get them ready for work, Master Chris walked to the stables and ordered himself a horse. It became clear to all that Master Chris was going to be involved in the work. As he rode alongside the Fito to oversee the work, he saw improvements that could be made to accommodate the slaves and to improve their work.

The next announcement took even the unbelievers in Master Chris's charge by surprise. He asked all the men and women who had a talent in craftsmanship to produce something to show him.

The men quickly made whatever they could with the meager materials they could collect. Master Chris selected various items that caught his eye and gave the Fito orders to take the pieces to sell at the market in Punda. The proceeds would go to each artist. The slave could use that money to buy their freedom. Soon the Master was overwhelmed with hats, cups, alpargatas (slipper-like shoes), decorative items, plates and bowls.

The unbelievers raised their voices. They were convinced the Master was going to keep all the money. They sat and sneered at the people who were willing to work long hours after their field work to produce more money for the Master. The population in the huts was divided on the matter.

Most of the people didn't know what to believe, but they gave it a try anyway. The believers worked harder than ever. Soon they needed a place to work on their art. Master Chris gave Fito permission for the men to use the stable to keep their supplies and to use makeshift tables to work on their projects.

Following that latest development, it became uncommonly quiet on the plantation. Even the unbelievers didn't dare to voice their opinions this time. Only one or two hard cases prophesied that the Master was 'up to something'.

But when the people received their first black coins, the profit from their own crafts and sales, it was settled. They were going to be free someday. They could earn their freedom now.

Mimina and Didi also made the most of this situation. In earnest, they began making soap, oil, flu medicine, and ointments and gave it all to Fito to sell for them. Fito found a lady in the market who would sell their products at her stall for a percentage of the price. The oils were especially in high demand.

When the medicine women received their first black coins, they danced around with them, the boys sharing in their happiness. Later there were also some ten-cent coins, some quarters, and eventually a silver guilder.

Now Mimina woke her sons an hour earlier every day. At four in the morning, they would start producing whatever they could sell in town.

"One day we will be free." Everybody used that phrase once or twice a day. Never in history had the work on the plantation been done so quickly and so well. The sooner the work was done, the sooner Fito would permit the men to break for the day and spend some time on their own projects.

The prayer group came together almost every day now. Their lips were praying while their hands were busy making their specialties. All had changed for Mimina. She went back to live in her old room. She expected to hear at any moment that the Master was going to be married. She never saw him privately now, and she could never ask him for any more privileges.

On a morning, she went to his library with a cup of coffee. She knocked and waited for permission. When inside she put the coffee down and stood in the slave position waiting for permission to speak.

"Mimina, what is it?" Master Chris asked.

"My lord, I wanted to ask permission for my sons to start going to Punda with the Fito so they can see how the selling of the products goes and learn from that. Could my lord give permission for that?"

"Good idea, Mimina, they need to know the city and understand how a market works. Why don't you go with them the first time so you can see your mother and maybe sell some things?" Master Chris's eyes were sparkling in his enthusiastic response. He continued, "Next time they could go with the Fito alone. What do you think?"

Mimina couldn't believe her luck. She received something from the Master without giving him anything back. How was it possible?

"Thank ... thank you, my lord." She stammered and took some steps towards the door.

Master Chris stood and his eyes met hers. He took a step forward and reached out for Mimina. Unexpectedly he pulled her into his arms and pressed his lips to her ears.

Mimina didn't know what to do. She wanted to pull free but liked the intimate gesture somehow. It felt good to be held again. She stood still and enjoyed the embrace for some time. She couldn't swear to it, but she thought she heard him talking in her ear. He kept repeating her name and said, "I love you." But, of course, that could not be true. A master never loved a slave.

"You take what you want; I take what I want too," she thought when she stood there and let the Master embrace her.

Master Chris pushed her a bit away from his chest and looked her in the face. He pressed his lips on her forehead and said, "Mimina, you are everything to me."

This time Mimina knew for real. She had heard correctly. She didn't have too much time to think about this new development. Master Chris pushed her from him and ran out of the library. He fled!

There was no other word to use.

The cup of coffee remained untouched on his table.

Chapter Twenty Four

Mimina's boys were growing in many ways now. After that first time they continued to go to Punda with Fito. They learned from the Fito in Punda how to do business. They could read and write and were used to keeping books and selling and buying products. They even went to Banda Bou, the countryside, to buy and sell. Robby, the oldest son, turned out to be dependable and served the Fito from Punda all the time. Jack and Ronny were strong and very good with numbers. The three were always together.

When they came back home after their travels, they brought many stories from their trips. Under the big tamarind tree, they would sit down and talk with the men, telling them what was going on with other slaves on other plantations. The boys told about plantations where slaves were severely beaten, malnourished, and mistreated. Nothing compared to their plantation. They told about mean Fitos, cruel masters, and difficult work conditions for the slaves. Circumstances on some of the plantations were so brutal that all children under five died from various causes. And the mothers didn't even mourn their children, for they would rather have them be with Jesus than living in such difficult situations.

The prayer group began to pray for the other plantations and asked God what could be done. They decided to put together small bags of produce and other goods and send these with the boys the next time they went to Banda Bou. Mai Sila sent flour bags for the women to make dresses. The boys made a batch of coconut oil to hand out. And some of the slaves who had nothing to send even gave some precious copper coins from their savings.

The prayer group committed themselves to pray for the other plantations and instructed the boys to bring the gospel to these slaves.

"Robby, you go and teach them to pray, so they can pray to God directly. Tell them about our hope in God. Don't be shy. Make them listen. They will be thankful when they understand."

Robby told the group about some slaves who worked in the salt mines. The combination of the sun and the salt made the people prone to wounds, infections, amputations, and eventually early death. The masters and the Fitos didn't care to improve their conditions. The families lived in a one-room hut with ten to fifteen people together. On some plantations, it was even against the law to pray. This news made the people realize the blessings they took for granted every day.

If they fell sick, they just called one of the medicine women, and they received care right away. Punishments were just and far between. Work was hard but there was always food to eat. Families had not been sold for years, and children could stay with their mothers, and even learn to read.

The most surprising news Robby and his brothers brought was the news of a man they met in Punda. He was a slave and worked on the slave boats, buying and selling slaves with his master. He traveled on the slave ship from Curaçao to New York, a city in America.

"The man told me," said Robby in a low voice, looking around to notice any eavesdroppers, "in America white people are fighting against white people to take away slavery."

This news astounded the hearers. How could that be true? Nobody spoke.

"There is even a white lady who wrote a book about a black slave, *Uncle Tom,* and it seems that everyone is reading that book," Robby said, as his brothers nodded in agreement.

"White people fighting slavery? Are you sure?" Adam could not believe his ears. He suspected the boys were telling tales, but he didn't dare to say so.

"I never thought white people, any white people, would care about black people. But I know my God. He is working on our behalf. I say, let's keep praying, friends. We are doing well. Things are moving. God has permitted us to hear these things today to have more courage to keep fighting in prayer," Ruben burst out, and the group hollered in agreement with him.

That night the boys' stories were told and retold in all the huts on the plantation. Even Mimina got to hear the news later that night. Of course, she wasn't in the prayer meeting but the boys brought her up to date.

They shared another important item of information with her.

"Mai, our Master makes a lot of money in Punda selling and buying cocoa from Venezuela. Our Master is very rich because of this cocoa. He buys it in Venezuela, grinds it in Punda, and sells it in small bags to Europe. He makes money like water."

"I wish we were in Venezuela. We could be producing and selling cocoa to people like him," Ronny said. "We could be free in a short amount of time. I am so tired of working so hard and making a few black coins at a time. At this rate, it will take us 20 years to buy freedom for ourselves and for you, Mai. And then we still have to worry about Mai Sila and Fito. They need to be freed too. We will be old and bent over by the time we are free and we will have to work to feed ourselves then."

In a couple of phrases, these intelligent boys summarized the problem they were facing. Their family was big and expensive. The price to buy their freedom would be double or triple the price of a regular slave. They would never be able to make enough to buy everyone's freedom.

Mimina had recognized this problem before but she didn't know what to do about it. Maybe this was the solution: if her boys could go to Venezuela and make more money there. If they could do that, they would be free men—young, healthy, free, and strong men—who could build a life for themselves.

Mimina talked about it tentatively with her mother, testing Didi's reaction. She expected preaching and a scolding, but instead she received understanding.

"How many times was I not ready to escape with you, my child? If your grandmother had let me, I would have tried and probably been killed trying. I understand your need to be free, even better than you realize."

They sent for Mai Sila from Punda, and for many nights they talked only about different ways to accomplish a successful escape.

Fito was let in on the scheme; he listened to all their plans until he was asked to actively participate in the planning.

"I don't know," he said, "I never have enabled a slave to escape. That is against the law and if they catch us, they will kill us."

All four of them remembered the incident with Master Thomas from the Plantation *Seru Haltu.* He came by with killer dogs, wanting to search the property for his two escaped slaves. Fito Adam denied him and his dogs entrance to the plantation, so Master Thomas used the lash on him. Someone hurriedly called Master Chris, who came to hear what it was all about.

"Thomas," he had said to the other master, "if I let you come onto my property with those dogs, you will upset all my slaves, and we are in the middle of harvest. We are working long hours to get every-thing in before the rains arrive. I cannot have this right now."

Master Thomas was very upset with Master Chris and they argued for a long time. Finally, Master Chris promised to send Fito with a search team to try to find the slaves. Master Chris gave his word that he would personally bring the escaped slaves, if caught, back to Master Thomas. That was the best that Mas-ter Thomas was going to get, so he left grudgingly.

As promised, Fito and his search team looked for the escaped slaves. They brought a big bag of food, beans, two hats, two pairs of new alpargatas, and two shirts with them. They left everything high on a rock so it could be clearly seen from all sides. They also brought a big calabash bowl with fresh water, two bottles of coconut oil, some soap, and some unleavened bread. They tied a milk goat and two bottles filled with clean water by a tree next to the rock.

The next day they went back to look and found everything gone except the milk goat. She had been milked though, and the calabash was found upside down on the rock.

With a sincere heart, Fito could tell his mas-ter that they found proof that somebody was in the woods but that they did not find the slaves. Master Chris sent a message for Master Thomas. And that was the end of it. After that, the relationship between the two plantations was never the same.

"Master Chris will never send dogs after Robby, Jacques, and Ronny." Mimina was convinced of that. "You need to help me to get my boys off the island. You need to help me. Look how big they already are. Look how much they know. They are valuable as slaves. They can be sold any minute. I cannot keep them in the house forever. They are not young kids anymore. They are men. They need to do men's work. I don't know how much longer it is gonna take for me to buy their freedom. I want them free now!"

Everybody understood Mimina's turmoil and they agreed to help her, even Fito. There followed a time of much planning, secret visits, scraping together money, and preparation.

Mai Sila was to find material to sew the boys proper free-man clothes which they would need in Venezuela. Mai Sila also bought the hats and the umbrellas that went with the clothes. Mimina sewed a heavy bag that was more or less waterproof for the boys to carry all their belongings.

Mimina made soap, oil, and packed small bags full of herbs for any imaginable disease her boys might encounter. Fito found out what the currency in Venezuela was and secretly bought pesos for the boys. He was also in charge of finding a captain that would accept the responsibility of taking the boys safely to Venezuela.

Mai Sila dried meat, dates, raisins, and nuts, and made flatbread cookies. She packed some calabashes for scooping water and to drink from. Using flour bags, Mimina sewed a bed that could be rolled out to sleep on.

The young boys prepared themselves as much as possible by learning about the new country of Venezuela and the cocoa trade. They already spoke reasonable Spanish. They also made pens and bought ink and paper so they could write from Venezuela.

All the preparations were very time-consuming and secretive. Mimina traveled twice to Punda to purchase needed articles for the trip. Finally, six weeks after the planning started, everything was ready.

The boys cried the last night they were at the plantation. The plan was for them to leave for Punda as they did on a regular workweek, but from there they would not return. They chose not to tell the other slaves goodbye. Not even the prayer group was informed, so as not to compromise them and put them in danger.

A captain of a small market boat would take the boys clandestinely to Venezuela.

"We are gonna be free, Mai," Jacques said through his tears. "Finally we are gonna be free."

They hugged their mother and grandmother.

"Mai, don't cry. We will send for you when we are good. We will send for all of you. We will all start fresh in a new country. We promise to work hard and save."

****

Nobody on the plantation was aware that the boys had left, so accustomed were they to the boys spending time in Punda. After a week, the tutor came to Master Chris to inquire about the boys. That was the fi rst time Chris heard that something might be going on.

"What do you mean, you don't know where the boys are?" Master Chris jumped up and leaned forward over his desk, facing his tutor. "Did something happen to them? Were they out of your sight? Are they not with Fito? Did they have their slave passes with them all the time? If something happens with those boys, Mimina will die."

"I really don't know what happened, Master. Fito sent them to Banda Bou, and I came back to the Plantation to continue teaching the kids here. When Fito arrived today without the boys I asked him about them, and he said they were here on the plantation with me. But I have been here a week and I have not seen them." The tutor was visibly shaken, knowing full well that he could be fi red for losing three of his pupils.

Where could the boys be?

Master Chris called immediately for Ruby. "Do you know where the boys are?" he asked Ruby.

"They are in town with their tutor, Master," she said. At the same moment she recognized the tutor and changed her response. "I don't know, Master."

"Please go get Mimina." Master Chris was surly.

It took a long time for Mimina to come. The two men sat in tense quietness.

"Master?" Mimina asked with an innocent voice.

"Where are the boys?" Master Chris asked pointedly. He was beginning to fear the worst, and somehow he felt Mimina was too smug and too innocent. He suspected that she knew something about what was going on.

Mimina stood in front of the desk in the slave position. Her thoughts were swirling as numerous scenarios fl ew by. The family had agreed to tell the Master that they didn't know about the boys' escape. This was to protect them and the Fito since helping slaves escape was a crime worthy of the same punishment that the actual runaway would get when captured.

Suddenly Mimina felt like telling the truth. She was not going to tiptoe around Master Chris anymore.

"Well?" he asked impatiently. "Do you know or not?"

"I do not know exactly, my lord, but last week I received notice that they have departed to Venezuela." Mimina spoke in a level voice, void of all emotions.

The Master became red in the face and jumped up when he heard the news. "You can go to your house," he barked at the tutor. "I will deal with you later. I don't understand how you could have lost three valuable, capable young men!"

As soon as the tutor left, Master Chris walked around the desk and grabbed Mimina. He pulled her close to him and screamed, "Woman, how could you do that to me? How could you send my sons far from me without telling me?"

Mimina's eyes were as big as saucers. "Your sons? I didn't know you saw my children as yours. You never told me that."

Completely upset, Master Chris hugged Mimina tight. With his hands, he loosened her braids and let her hair fall thick and black on her back. He pushed his face into her hair and said with a muffl ed voice, "Woman, don't you know how much I love you? How much I love my sons? Why did you do this to me? I would have done anything you wanted for them, but why send them away? Don't you know how danger- ous the trip is? How many don't make it? How dan- gerous South America is? Aye, Mimina, aye, Mimina, what have you done?"

Mimina felt his tears on her neck, dripping down her back. She was crying too.

For the fi rst time since she came to Master Chris voluntary, she hugged him with the intention of comforting him instead of getting something from him.

"You knew my children were slaves. I don't want that anymore. My great-grandmother prayed for our freedom, my grandmother is still praying, and so is my mother. I need to make it happen. I need to make sure my kids will not be slaves anymore. I need to do it. They need to be free men. Maybe their life will be hard, but at least it is their life, not the

Master's possession."

"But they are my children too, Mimina."

"I didn't know that you felt that way, Master Chris. They have never received a fatherly hug or any kind of affection from you. They are still slaves under the law. I have heard that other masters have given their slave sons their freedom. You didn't behave like a father to my way of thinking."

"But I don't want my children to be slaves either!" Master Chris declared.

"What?" Mimina couldn't believe her ears. "You don't want them to be slaves? Don't you sign their slave pass every week giving them permission to travel to town and back? Don't you own them? How do you mean you don't want them to be slaves? They ARE slaves, your slaves, and you have not done anything about it. Why didn't you free them if you loved them so much?"

"Free them? And where would they live? What would they eat? Could I keep them under my roof if they were free? Who would have taken care of their education? I was just waiting for them to be grown up to give them their freedom, when they could work and provide for themselves. I cannot free you. You are not mine. I don't have any papers for you. My father doesn't want to set you free either. But I could free the boys. I have their birth certifi cates. I took care of them their whole lives. I would want to... to... marry you if you were not a slave anymore."

Mimina couldn't believe her ears. She could have received freedom for her sons if she had been more patient? She just used her life savings and those of her family to send her boys on a dangerous adventure, while Master Chris would have granted it for free?

Master Chris kissed her ears, neck, and face. She felt his tears mingling with hers. His mouth found hers and he pressed himself to her. She felt how eager he was. Suddenly, he released her from his tight grip and ran out of the room. He fl ed... Again...

Mimina was left alone in his study. She dropped on her knees and sobbed inconsolable. She saw her empty life for what it was. Since she was fi fteen she was always working and thinking of ways to improve her family's living conditions. She had put her boys before all her own needs and wants. She had slept over and over again with the Master to get what she needed for her boys. Now she had lost her boys, the reason for her life. Her future looked bleak. No boys to look after and to care for. No boys to scheme for. She lost the ability to care for anyone other than her boys. Would she die a lonely, bitter woman?

In those seconds, her life passed before her eyes. She did not have a husband; she sent her kids to a strange country; and if it was as dangerous as the Master said, she would never see them again. She did not have a church; the love of God was far off. She could see herself becoming old, serving the slaves when they were sick, cleaning the Master's house, and dying a slave. No future, no hope, no love, no fulfi llment. Mimina hit rock bottom. The old, proud Mimina would have cut her tongue off instead of praying, but in that moment of complete darkness she pressed three simple words out of her hoarse throat.

"God, help me."

Chapter Twenty Five

The next day Master Chris left for Punda, and he didn't come back. The plantation was buzzing. It had leaked out that the boys were missing, and speculations were flying around.

"Mimina, I think we need to tell our friends what is going on. Some of the people are really concerned. They believe the boys are sold. Let's talk with them and tell them the truth so they can pray for the boys," Didi suggested.

Fito was called and told about the boys' escape. He was distressed to hear it but understood the reasons for doing it. "I was going to send Ruben away too when he was younger. I would have done it if we couldn't have come to live on this plantation.

We've had it so much better with this Master and Fito than we ever had in our life, so I decided to stay put and wait."

Mimina felt ashamed when she heard the plantation described in such terms. Since the time when the boys came back with their stories of other plantations, she had been thinking the same thing. It was a good life on this plantation. If only they could have been free.

Fito took it upon himself to talk with the prayer group and tell them what was going on and asked for prayer for the boys. And that evening, for the first time in her adult life, Mimina set foot in a prayer meeting again. She huddled close to her mother and didn't say anything. But her friends were all happy to see her.

Master Chris stayed six weeks in Punda. Fito told them that the rift between father and son was breached, but other than that, no news came from Punda until Chris sent word to prepare a guest room. He came back with two big surprises. First of all, he brought Yùfrou Miriam with him. She was accompanied by her husband and her little daughter, a spitting image of herself at that age.

Mimina fell in love with that little girl right away. She brought back pleasant memories of her own carefree early years when she ran around with Miriam. The family was to stay a week on the plantation. Miriam was eager to see everyone and introduce her husband. And she wanted to show her husband and daughter everything at the place where she had grown up. She was bubbling with happiness and eagerness.

Mimina served the table on this special occasion, and deep in her heart she confessed she wanted to hear what was going on in Miriam's life, since she had been her best and only friend. She was amazed to realize that the hatred she had felt for Miriam was now gone. In its place there was a void. She didn't feel the love or the hatred of the past. A sense of peace came over her. Was God healing her heart?

With her eyes cast down and her head lowered, she stood at the door of the dining room and waited for the family to dine. When she noticed that the child liked the fried potatoes Mai Didi made, she helped her with a second portion.

She refilled Mijnheer Frederick's cup of coffee and poured a glass of cold lemonade for Miriam. "Oh, how I missed Mai Yeye's recipe for lemonade. Nobody could make it like hers, except you, Sila and Didi of course." Miriam laughed and gave her husband her glass so he could taste it.

Miriam talked without ceasing. She brought news and greetings from many people Master Chris knew when he was living in Europe. She told about places they had visited and family members they had seen. The dinner was a pleasant one, and Mimina listened intently to the details of Miriam's life.

After dinner the family stood up to leave, and Mimina hovered close by to clean up the table. She was totally unprepared for what would happen next.

Miriam reached out to her and hugged her, saying, "Mimina, I missed you." It was just like those horrible years of animosity between them didn't exist anymore. With that hug and smile, they were transported back to a date before the beating, before the master-slave period. Mimina didn't ... couldn't ... say anything.

"Tonight I want you to come to the porch because I have something to tell you. Come as soon as we finish dinner." With those words, the family went to their room to enjoy a well-deserved siesta and escape the heat of the day.

The other big surprise came after lunch when Master Chris sent for her in his study. Mimina glanced at him before lowering her eyes and waiting. He was dressed in his professional town clothes, and he looked important and a little intimidating to Mimina, especially when he sat behind that big desk, going through some paperwork that also looked important.

"I want you to help me find the boys and bring them back," Master Chris announced abruptly. "It is too dangerous in Venezuela, and I cannot let them stay there. I have found a boat with a captain and a private investigator. He will track them down and bring them back. It would be much easier if you would give me all the information you have. Like possible contact persons, the name of the captain that took them, the boat they went on, the place they are heading for. I don't expect them to have an address there, do they?"

Master Chris's voice was serious and determined. He meant business.

Mimina's heart skipped a beat. Her legs felt wobbly. She sat down on the edge of the closest chair. With her hands on the desk, she steadied herself. She had not expected this news. She looked the

Master squarely in the face, scrutinizing his eyes and his features to get more information. She saw tenderness, seriousness, commitment. What she saw made her heart skip another beat. She could not believe her eyes. Shame, as never before, filled her. She had always used this man. She had deprived him of a fair try at his marriage, deprived him of healthy children with his wife. After the way she had treated her Master, milking him for her boys and a better life, he sat there and showed ... love?

Her heart told her to trust Master Chris, so she told him all she knew, which was not much, about the travels of the boys.

****

As if all that were not enough, Master Chris had more news. "I called you here to tell you that on the island of French Saint Martin slaves are receiving their permanent freedom this week. The people have been preparing for abolition some years now. When I was in Punda, I spoke with different people about this situation, and I am informed that a coalition had been sent to Europe to talk to Dutch King Wilhelmus regarding the abolition of slavery here on the island of Curacao."

Mimina's hand flew to her mouth. A groan escaped her.

Master Chris continued, "There is a committee appointed to talk with all the different stakeholders. They spoke with leaders of the Catholic Church, with the Domi, with the traders, and when I was in town they interviewed me as a plantation owner. I think slavery is almost over now, Mimina."

****

After work, Mai Didi, Mai Sila and Mimina called Fito into the kitchen to tell him the good news. They were talking and laughing at the same time. Nobody could make coherent sentences. Mai Didi sent for Ruben, and the prayer group came hurriedly together in the kitchen, since the women were on duty with guests in the house and could not leave. After hearing the news and enjoying a piece of fresh apple pie, they left.

Soon the horns started blowing, sharing the good news or just making a happy noise. Under the cover of the early night, a slave from a nearby plantation came to ask what was going on. A free black man walked in and asked the same. Soon they left to bring the good news to other plantations. Then the tambu song started. It was loud and festive around the slave huts. The people sang:

Kaiman djuku	Black djaku
Djuku kaiman	Djaku Crocodile
Mi n'ta laba tayó	I will not wash any dishes
Mi n' ta laba kònchi mas	I will not wash any bowl
Mi n' ta bari kas mas	I will not broom your house
Mi no ta katibu di Master mas	I am not a slave anymore

People were dancing and the drums became louder and louder. Fresh corn was thrown on a fi re and more tambu was made up.

Libertat galité	*Freedom Galite*
Master muhé mes lo laba tayó	*Mefrou can wash her own plates*
Libertat galité	*Freedom Galite*
Pushi mes lo laba tayó	*The cat can wash her own plate*
Libertat galité	*Freedom Galite*
Master hòmber mes lo laba koprá.	*The Master can do his own work*

Mimina could not go to any of the activities on the plantation. She could hear the drums in the night air, but she stayed to clean up after dinner so Mai Didi could go. She couldn't leave the house anyway since Miriam wanted to talk with her on the porch. She planned to hear Miriam out. She had washed her thin white cotton dress and pressed it earlier. She wanted to be prepared for whatever Miriam had to say.

On the porch, Miriam was all by herself. Master Chris took her husband into the library to talk, and Ruby was with the little child in her room. Miriam was waiting for Mimina. She wanted Mimina to sit, but Mimina chose to stand, not daring to forget for one minute who she was.

When Miriam started talking, Mimina lowered herself onto a chair anyway. Her already wobbly legs would not have carried her for sure.

"I went back to the church in the Netherlands," Miriam said. "I was invited to a prayer group for women and I accepted. My husband made me go. In the beginning, I went just to meet people, but later I started liking it. The group prayed a lot for the slaves and the abolition of slavery. It made me think. I told them I owned you, and just saying those words in

Europe sounded wrong. I shouldn't own somebody else. We are all God's children."

Mimina forgot to breathe for a minute. Then the air escaped her loudly.

Miriam continued, "We are all writing letters now to politicians, putting pressure on the government for abolition." Miriam stopped talking and looked at Mimina.

She continued, "Last week in Punda I went to a meeting with the same goal. We prayed and wrote letters. Most of the women in this meeting are white people, but last week we received our first two black members into the prayer group."

Tears started coursing down Mimina's cheeks. She had no idea where they came from. She sniffed and dabbed them with a paper towel. She wasn't prepared for this.

Miriam came closer to her and pulled her from the chair. She gave Mimina a big hug and said, "I never asked you forgiveness for what I did when we were young. It was a shameful thing to do. I was a jealous girl. I am sorry. I already asked God to forgive me, so now I am asking you."

Mimina could not find words, but hugged her former friend and found that words were not necessary. Before Mimina knew it, she was telling Miriam about her fabulous sons—how they looked, how smart they were, what they learned, and also how they fled the island and tried to start over in Venezuela as free men.

"Oh Mimina. That is so hard. You haven't seen your sons in all this time, have not heard from them? Nothing? Can't Chris do something?"

"He is sending an investigator to try to find them. I made a lot of mistakes, Miriam. I made my sons my god. I worshipped them. I lived for them and forgot to give thanks to God for all we had. I was always bitter because of what we didn't have."

Chapter Twenty Six

In her room that night, a humbled but happy Mimina lowered herself to the floor and wept before God.

The next morning, before 4 A.M., she woke her mother. What a relief to finally confess, "Mai, I am sorry for all I have put you through. I was a bad daughter, causing you all that heartache. Can you forgive me?"

Didi hugged her daughter and cried. "Daughter, you cannot imagine how proud you make me today. My God is good. I have prayed for you my whole life. And here you are, a grown-up woman with sons. It took a long time but here you are. I will send word for Mai Sila today. It is the happiest day of my life."

That very same day Mimina went to the prayer meeting and asked them to pray for her relationship with God.

****

The rainy season was approaching quickly and the night air turned cold. Mimina talked with Master Chris and he gave permission for the people to use the storage room for meetings when it rained or was too cold. Some free black people came to the prayer meeting and asked for prayer. They were seeking fellowship and people to pray with.

They told about the horrific situations they lived in. Although they were now free, life was not any better for many of them. There were no homes or work available for free black people who were mostly unskilled laborers. The masters would rather buy a field slave than hire a free man and pay him every day. These people were suffering from hunger, and most of their children were sick. Although they rented some small houses to live in, they were infested with insects, and many times the children went to bed hungry.

The slaves could not believe the hardships of the free black people. They had been so keen on freedom for so long that they had never thought that freedom could be so difficult.

Mimina spoke with Master Chris and got his approval for her plan. She gathered all the people together in one big meeting and invited the free black men to come back and tell their story to all the slaves. Their stories made the people quiet and pensive. So freedom had big dangers too. So what now?

A long discussion followed about how to be better prepared for the coming freedom. They all agreed that everyone would need to have a skill. Many planned to keep making their crafts when they were free. When the free blacks heard about the handicraft project, they wanted to join; however, they had no one to sell their products for them in town.

They could not read or write so doing business was difficult. The result often was that they had materials left over that they could not sell. Mimina got permission from Master Chris for the free blacks to use the work space on the plantation to make handcrafts that Fito could sell in town, thus improving their income.

Mimina, Mai Sila, and Didi started to make big amounts of coconut oil to sell. The demand in town was growing, and people sent word with Fito to send different combinations of coconut oil. The proceeds of this product were destined especially for the free brothers who could not care for their family.

One day Shon Pai came by Mai Didi's kitchen to ask for Mimina. He was a thin, black free man, an active member of the prayer meetings. Mai Didi gave him a cup of coffee and a sandwich. He was depressed, because his six-year-old granddaughter was sick with fever. She hadn't moved from her mat for several days. He feared for her life and wanted Mimina to go with him to check on her.

"It is almost two hours walking to my house," he apologized.

Didi was surprised with that. "Two hours walking and still you come here to work and to pray with us?"

"Didi, I don't know what to do anymore. My wife died ten years ago. My only living daughter became sick with the flu last year and left her six-year-old daughter for me. My mother lives with us, and all three of us are hungry. When I come to this plantation the prayer friends lift me up. I feel hope to be worshipping with people that believe like I do. And sometimes they give me some corn, some rice, or some beans. It helps me to provide for my family.

"Now I can work in the shop. I am sure God put me on this path so I could meet all of you. And I am thankful for that."

He laughed and for a moment Didi could see the carefree man he was, beneath all the hardships he was experiencing. He raised his cup of coffee and saluted Didi. "And you make a mean cup of coffee. Is it okay with your master to give it to a black man?"

Didi laughed too. She sat down and took a cup for herself. "This coffee is from Colombia. They make good coffee there. Our Fito brings us a package every now and then. Not even the Master have such good coffee. And I only use it for very special occasions. That is one of the blessings of selling in the market. You get to buy too."

At that moment, Mimina came back to the kitchen. She was a bit taken aback, seeing her mother sitting there, seemingly carefree and laughing and talking with a man.

As soon as Shon Pai saw Mimina, he jumped up, took a big gulp from his remaining coffee, and walked to the door, thanking Mai Didi again. The problem was explained to Mimina, and it was agreed that she would go with Shon Pai to help his ill grand-daughter.

Before they could get away, however, Mai Didi hurried to the annex and gathered up a big ham, potatoes, corn, onions, and green pepper to give to him. "Shhh," she said when he started protesting. "Mimina will straighten it all out with the Master later. She can get whatever she wants from him. And if it is for a good goal, our Master will go along. He is not the worst."

When their new friend was reluctant to take everything, Didi thought of a compromise: "You can come and clean out the pig stall for me next week as payment. I am getting too old for that now. I could use some help."

Mimina had permission to use the open wagon, and she helped the boy to saddle the horse. She confessed to Shon Pai that she was not an experienced driver.

They both laughed. "Neither am I, Miss Mimina," he said. "I have been on a wagon a total of four times in my life and all the times, it was when I was sold from one master to another. But we will make do. The horse looks tame enough to me. And it will help me get quickly to my baby. My mother will be frantic by now taking care of her alone. Miss Mimina, you drive and I will pray."

Mimina threw her bag of medicines into the wagon and hopped in. She checked to make sure she had her slave pass with her. A black woman on a wagon would attract attention for sure. Thank God, the horse did what he was supposed to do without her guiding him too much. She made a mental note to ask the stable boys to teach her more soon. But for now, she had no choice.

In less than half an hour, they arrived at the compound where the free blacks were allowed to live. It was close to a warehouse where many of them found day jobs. The living conditions were even more horrible than Shon Pai had described. The streets were muddy pools, and the homes were small huts constructed of whatever material they could find, including mud and grass. Shon Pai's house was small and hot. The smell of sickness greeted Mimina at the door.

Shon Pai's mother came out right away and took Mimina's hands. Tears filled her eyes when she saw the food.

Thank God, the house had windows. Right away and against the elderly lady's wishes, Mimina opened the window and let the air flow into the hut. And she needed the daylight to examine the sick child. Grandma boiled water and made some tea for the child. It was obvious she had a bad case of influenza, a sickness that killed many children and elderly folks.

Mimina left Grandma with detailed instructions on the teas to give the child. She also left her with a supply of enough to last several days. The girl was to drink only boiled water from now on, and four times a day Grandma was supposed to give her the special blend of tea.

Shon Pai was very thankful for Mimina's services and felt bad that he could not pay her. "Anytime you need help, you call on me, Miss Mimina," he kept repeating. "I might be poor but I know how to be thankful to good folks who help me in time of need. I will come by on Sunday to tell you how the child is doing."

The next afternoon, after Mimina had her first driving class with the stable boy, she decided to drive out to the compound again. She stopped in the fields and took two huge watermelons with her. She drove slowly to the compound and learned how to work her way through the mud without getting stuck, just as the stable boy was teaching her.

Several people who had heard about her coming out to help Shon Pai's daughter greeted her warmly as she entered. Word went around quickly in the compound.

On Friday, she visited Shon Pai's family again and found the sick child sitting up and eating. She had good color and no fever. The worst was over.

Mimina gave them a bag of green beans she had picked that morning. The next day, while driving slowly through the compound, she was stopped by a wrinkled old lady who was missing most of her teeth.

"Miss Mimina, I know you helped Shon Pai's little granddaughter. Could you please come help my family too? We all have the same symptoms. I am afraid my grandchildren are gonna die if I can't find them some medicine." She opened her hand and showed Mimina two black coins. "I can give you these," she said hopefully.

Of course, Mimina was quick to take a look and ordered the room cleaned before she could do anything. She knew it was difficult for the people to find water to clean with, but she insisted. Soon some of the boys ran to the stream, more than an hour away, to bring back enough water to clean the house.

In the meantime, Mimina visited Shon Pai's daughter for the last time and declared her healed. She went back to the house of elderly Chela and tended to the sick children. All of them were naked and lying on dirty rags. They were so needy, and Mimina's heart went out to them. She made a mental note to bring some water next time and bathe the children properly. Also, she would see if Mai Didi had some leftover flour bags in the kitchen that she could wash and bring along.

That is how Mimina's ministry began. After a long talk with Master Chris about the needs of the free slaves, she received permission to use the wagon to visit them as often as necessary. The word went out about her skills, and soon other plantation owners dealing with the same flu among their people sent for Mimina and Didi.

When plantation owners paid them, Master Chris permitted them to keep the money as part of their savings. Mimina and Didi were excited. They used the money to buy flour sacks in Punda and some cheap white cotton to make sheets for the babies. Mimina bought bananas, rice, and beans in Punda for Fito to bring when he came back. Master

Chris permitted them to take to the compound all the bruised or damaged vegetables which were not needed in the slave huts.

Mimina became a woman of prayer. She prayed constantly for her sons, who still had not been located. Her hope was now in God, and she did not permit depression to defeat her.

She used her testimony to tell whoever would listen how she had lived before she gave God His rightful place, and how she had sent her boys to South America and lost them anyway. Her mother's heart moved her to pray for them continually.

Master Chris received report after report from the private investigator, but there was still no trace of the boys. After two years of continual prayer, Mimina and the family were expecting that at any time they would hear the worst.

Chapter Twenty Seven

On the island of Curacao, under the hot sun of the Caribbean, nature kept its slow pace, undisturbed by political battles regarding skin color. Days were filled with sun and nights full of stars.

At the south side of the island, the beautiful blue waves rippled the sandy white beaches. Coconut trees fanned the air lazily. In the countryside at Banda Bou, the slaves worked harder than ever. Masters tried to get their land farmed before the slaves were declared free.

In Punda, the discussion about abolition reached its highest point and tempers were flaring. Those against abolition considered their slaves their personal property, their investment, and were not going to stand by and let the government take them from them. Those who were working to form policies to apply after abolition was a reality were labeled nikker-lovers. Both sides felt unsafe, and physical attacks escalated.

Rumors among the slave population circulated continually with no one being sure of the facts. Some said the government was planning to buy all the slaves from the masters and then set them free. Others thought the slave owners would set them free and then demand that they work for them ten more years to pay back their initial debts. Everyone was on edge.

As time went by, feelings of desperation grew. The planting and harvesting seasons came and went without word of freedom. Those who just couldn't wait any longer bolted, risking all to go to Venezuela. Some died on the way, while others made it all the way there, only to realize that they were now slaves to poverty.

Every time Mimina heard of a slave leaving for Venezuela, she sent descriptions of her sons along with a promise of a handsome reward if they were found. But no word came. No response.

After two years, Master Chris sent another investigator to Venezuela, determined to find his sons. This time he found a Venezuelan investigator who might be more aware of hiding places where the boys might be living. Once again the prayer group doubled their prayers. After almost a year, the investigator came back to the island with a negative report. No luck. It looked like the boys had evaporated.

Mimina, at peace with God, stayed calm. "I will see my boys again," she kept repeating. "I will need to trust God harder."

Mimina and Master Chris developed a beautiful friendship over the years. They learned to know each other as persons and to appreciate each other's talents. There was nothing left of the relationship of master and slave. There was nothing left of the sinful relationship either. Anxiously they awaited the day of abolition so they could move forward with their hopes.

After one more fruitless meeting with the Catholic Bishop in Punda to hear how things were going, Chris made a decision. The waiting was too long. Why not move to America? Couldn't he pass Mimina off for a white person from Spain or the Middle East? He could marry her and live a peaceful, quiet life there. He could sell his assets on the island and move his cocoa business with him to the USA.

He laid his plans before Mimina, but she was totally against it!

For the first time in years, the former lovers, now friends, had a major falling out. "I'm not fleeing," Mimina said, digging in her heels. "Mai Sila is old. She will not be with us much longer. Mai Didi is healthy and all, but she would not have any family left here. And I don't want to live a life of lying if we are Christians. I want to trust God this time."

Master Chris had had enough. He asked Master Moron to come to the plantation so he could speak with him.

"Father, I have decided to take action. I love Mimina. I know you don't approve because she is black and a slave. But I have loved her my whole life. She is the mother, slave or not, of my three sons. I want to be more in her life. I cannot wait for abolition anymore. I am going to relocate and take Mimina with me. If need be, I will take the whole family and Fito with me. I want Mimina."

The news hit Master Moron hard. His face turned pale and the veins on his forehead stood out.

"Are you out of your mind, Chris?" Master Moron shouted. "You have been in her tangles too long now. She is nothing more than a slave. I don't care if you have children with her or not. Most masters have children with more than one slave. You don't see them marrying their slaves, do you?

This is insane. You will be the laughingstock of the whole city. And people will find out. Oh yes, believe me, they will find out and laugh at you."

Chris listened to all his father's arguments; he knew them by heart, and he would not be persuaded by them. He had made his decision and it was only a question of how to carry it out.

"Father, I can do it and I will do it. Grandpa Pe left this plantation under your care for me until I came of age. So it is mine to decide what I want to do with it. If I want to sell it off, that is my prerogative. And I don't want you to speak like that about Mimina. She is all I have. I love her and I will marry her any day now. If you cannot respect her, I will not be talking to you anymore."

"If you don't put this nonsense out of your head, you will not be my son anymore!" Master Moron left the room with his last words ringing in his son's ears.

Later that night Chris went to look for his father on the porch.

"Papa, how many times have you told me how good the medicine women have been for us? How they took care of me and Miriam—even saved my life when I was a baby? Their family cared for Grandmother Jana, for Grandfather Pe, for Grandmother Jo, for Miriam, for me. And let's not forget how they cared for Mom. Do you really think they are just slaves, Pa?"

Master Chris looked his father squarely in the face, but Master Moron could not face him. He looked away.

He heaved a big sigh and tried again to reason with Chris.

"Son, this is not the way we do things. I think I left you too long in that liberal Netherlands. You were changed when you came back. Just like your mother, you turned soft on me. Now you want to do the honorable thing for the slaves. And that is commendable. I do too. I never order them beaten, I feed them well, and I give them rest. But they are slaves, just slaves, people from Africa. They cannot live on their own if we don't help them. Our task is to care for them, coach them, and treat them as we would treat a child. We don't expect them to grow up and be fully the same as us, do we? They wouldn't know how to. They are ignorant people, good people of course. Most of our slaves are just good people, and I have been blessed to have them. The medicine women are the best! But to marry one? Come on... Chris. Let me find you a nice lady in town and you can keep your Mimina on the side if you want."

"I know this is not the way you do things, Papa, but there is a new generation out there. More and more people realize that black people are just that—black, but still people. If you really love me, Papa, I ask you to set Mimina free now so we do not need to wait for abolition. Give her and her family a letter of freedom. I will speak with them so they will not leave you, if that is what is holding you back. I will offer them good payment so they will stay. Please give me a letter of freedom for all three medicine women and their kids and husband. They deserve it. They earned it. I cannot wait any longer, Papa. I am not going to change; this is the life I want. I don't care about hypocritical white masters that sleep with their slaves and make babies and then look down on those same people. I don't see them going out and make babies with dogs or horses. They do it with slave girls because they know these are people, God's people. I broke with that sin, Papa. I made my peace with God. I have not touched Mimina again after I promised to God that I would not. It's not because she is not good enough but because she is too good. She is a better person than many white people I know in Punda."

"Oh my God, those are the exact words your mother used so many years ago..." Master Moron's voice trailed off. His face twisted. He opened his mouth to say something but didn't utter a word. Master Moron pulled at his beard, something he always did when he was agitated or nervous. He also ran his fingers through his hair.

"What is it, Papa?"

The silence was so heavy Chris could feel it. He noticed that his father was having an internal conflict. He let his father think it out in his own time. The silence stretched to five, and eventually to fifteen minutes. Suddenly Master Moron made a decision and plunged ahead.

He opened the antique desk that had been handed down from generation to generation, the same desk Master Chris used every day. What Master Chris didn't know was that it had a secret compartment under the drawer. With wide eyes, he saw how his father fidgeted with the drawer until a spring opened and a blue envelope was revealed.

His father gave the envelope to Chris, who reached out for it. A strange foreboding lurched around Chris's heart. He felt cold. His fingers trembled when he tried to open the letter. The paper was faded and thin. It was a very old letter.

Master Chris focused on the name on the envelope. "Papa, it is written by Grandpa Pe. I recognized his handwriting. Why are you giving me this?"

"Open it and read it for yourself," his father said. "Don't be too angry with me, son. I did what I thought was the best for all of us. With your mother sick and your sister's hysteria, I had nothing else I could do."

Now Master Chris became more curious. He opened the envelope and carefully removed the thin paper.

Master Moron fell into a chair and sat with his head in his hands, staring at the floor, while Chris began reading.

The words didn't make sense to him.

"...Master Jan brought the women... asked me to keep them for him... he was the illegitimate father of Didi... I learned later... he never came back for her... he died... his wife died... no family left... the women are not slaves... Never saw a letter of slavery... Nobody can claim ownership... Didi is a white man's daughter... set them free..."

"Does this say what I think it is saying?" Chris's controlled voice was frighteningly low. His face was constricted, red, and upset. "Mimina is not a slave? She doesn't belong to anybody? How could you have given her as a child to Miriam? She was not yours to give. Do you know how Miriam treated her? And all the time she was a free woman? How could you let her work for us, not paying her, treating her as a slave?"

Master Moron lowered his head. He tried to explain again, but his son was not listening anymore.

Master Chris paced. Suddenly a new thought hit him. "Are you telling me my sons are not slaves but free men? O... God... God... I... I could have married Mimina years ago and lived a normal life with my children?"

Master Chris shook his head to clear his jumbled thoughts, but to no avail. He walked away. Ruby, who was just walking by, was pushed aside rudely. Master Moron followed his son. Chris slammed the bedroom door in his face.

Master Moron knocked loudly and demandingly on the door, imploring his son to open it. Ruby, curious to see what was going on, raced to Mimina.

Master Moron heard the alarming sound of things crashing and glass breaking. Using all his force, he managed to break the door open. He ducked quickly when he saw an object flying toward his head. A vase scattered at his feet, barely missing him. Then he heard a chair crashing against the wall. He jumped out of the room.

Mimina came running and looked the situation over. "We'd better let him cool down, Master Moron," she advised. "This never happened before and I think something big is going on."

That whole day, nobody dared to knock or open the door again. Late in the afternoon, when it had been quiet for a long time, Mimina pushed the door ajar. She saw Master Chris on the floor, sleeping off his rage. He looked spent. His hands were bloody and his shirt was ripped. His room was trashed.

Very slowly, Mimina stepped over Chris and straightened up the room a little. She picked the broken glass up and moved the broken chairs and table out of the room to be repaired. Then she lowered herself to tenderly touch his face. He woke up slowly and reached for her. They embraced for a long time. Chris opened Mimina's hair and let it fall over her back.

He loved her long, flowing hair. It made her look so young and beautiful. How was he going to tell her what he had just learned? Could he hold it back for one more minute? She deserved to know. He kissed her. Really kissed her. He enjoyed her lovely presence for a few more minutes, knowing full well that these might be the last.

Mimina wriggled herself free from him, because the situation was quickly escalating, their intense feelings for each other once again awakened.

To get a breath, she walked to the kitchen searching for new lamps to replace the broken ones. She knew Chris liked to read at night.

She wanted to know why Chris behaved like that, but she didn't dare ask. She would give him time to collect his thoughts and tell her what the fight was about. It was probably about wanting to marry her, she thought.

However, she was completely unprepared for the news she and Didi received the next morning. They were both in a state of shock. How do you react when someone confesses to having stolen your life? Your LIFE?

Mai Yeye died believing herself a slave, and all the time she was free. Mai Sila was in Punda and didn't have a clue that she was a free woman.

Suddenly Mimina jumped up. "Oh my boys, my boyyyyyyyssssss...."

A heartbreaking sob escaped her and she fell to the floor in a faint. Master Chris could not comfort her. This was too huge.

He helped Mai Didi bring her to her room, and for the first time in his life, he saw the dark, stuffy room where the women had lived all these years. He lowered Mimina onto her mattress on the floor and wept openly.

Later that night Mai Didi and Mimina could talk. But words wouldn't come. Instead, they clung to each other silently.

Chapter Twenty Eight

As usual, Mimina and her mother got up early the next morning and carried water to the Big House. What else were they supposed to do? This news was so shocking, and they were not prepared to receive it. The routine of doing their usual tasks brought a sense of security, so they started preparing breakfast. Their future was wide open in front of them. But where to go? Where to live? How to proceed? They sent for Mai Sila and Fito.

Mai Didi and Mimina cleaned the rooms and made the beds just as they always had.

As they worked, the tears kept falling.

"Mai Yeye didn't know," Didi said sadly.

Mimina nodded. The old rage against the white race returned full force in her heart. She almost gagged on her hate. But she hid her feelings from her mother and kept working quietly.

Later that day, they called Ruben and Adam to give them the shocking announcement. The news came like a bombshell.

Mimina walked with her head down around the plantation. She could not feel happy for the news. The way it came about was too painful.

Finally, after two days, Mai Sila arrived. Her strength helped both the ladies come back to reality. When she heard the news, she sat down. She kept asking for reassurance.

"Are you sure, Didi? How is it possible?"

Mai Sila stayed a couple of days at the plantation and went with Mimina to visit those who were ill. She noticed the old hatred was consuming Mimina again. She saw how the enemy was winning territory in her granddaughter again.

She said, "Mimina, remember we are not to judge. We cannot allow bitterness to reign in our heart."

Mimina lashed out, "I wish Master Moron would drop dead. May the devil have his soul! He called us black. His own soul is black. He will fry in hell for what he did to us. He let Mai Yeye die without knowing the truth; she believed God had not answered her prayers. All the time she was a free woman."

Barely controlling her rage, Mimina picked up a stick and threw it forcefully into the woods. She stood with her back to her grandmother.

"I hate them all."

Mai Sila rushed to her side and exclaimed, "I used to be exactly as you! I hated them too. But Mai Yeye asked me one day if I was without sin. If I would dare to throw the first stone at them? I couldn't honestly throw that stone, Mimina, since I had sinned many times. So I made a decision to leave their punishment to God. He will judge. I can't.

"I want to ask you today, have you never done something to somebody that you regret? Think of your sons, you insisted on sending them to Venezuela. They might come back and blame you for it. Or they might die and you would be responsible somehow."

A concerned Mai Sila called Ruben for a special prayer meeting that night, and their other friends eagerly joined them. Some wanted to hear the details of what happened, but it was still too painful to talk about. How to start a new life? A life stolen from you by people you trusted? Could they really learn to forgive? Mimina couldn't forgive. No, she didn't even want to try.

In the prayer group, Ruben spoke about the boy Joseph of the Bible, who was sold into slavery by his brothers. He lived his whole life as a slave and even spent some years in prison for things he didn't do. Even in slavery, God had a plan for Joseph. Ruben called the women to look for God in this situation and forgive the masters. He promised that

God would make something good come out of this situation too.

Everybody was touched by this biblical parallel which nobody had seen before. The women and their friends held hands and asked God to help them all to forgive. They were all "Josephs" in this country.

Mimina was greatly moved by Ruben's words. Shame filled her heart. She sat down, trembling. The hundreds of cups of black bark tea she made for *Mefrou* Amy passed before her eyes. It was as if she could see the cups and smell the tea, and *Mefrou*'s face had never been so clear before her.

"Can you throw the first stone?" Mai Sila's voice came back to her. Strange—it sounded like the Lord's voice.

Did *Mefrou* suffer when month after month she didn't become pregnant? Mimina could still see *Mefrou* Amy sitting alone in her room, day after day. Did she not rob Chris of a chance to have children with his wife? What if that tea had killed *Mefrou*? Wasn't Mimina just as sinful as they were?

She wrapped her face in her hands and cried out to God, asking Him to forgive her.

Astonished, her family rushed to her and tried to understand what was going on. Mimina could not explain, her deep conviction of sin touched her so deeply. She went to her mat, lay on her back, and stared with wide open eyes.

****

Master Moron left for town. He sent word with Ruby that he would do whatever was in his power to compensate them for what had happened.

In her heart, Mimina knew what she was to do. It was time to come clean. If Chris confessed his family's sins, she certainly could confess hers.

The next day she went to the library and asked Chris for permission to talk. His eyes brightened. Hope shone. Eagerly he pulled out a chair and waved Mimina to sit.

"Mimina, I am so sorry..." he started to say, but now it was time for Mimina to wave him to be still.

"I need to tell you something." She lowered her head in her hands and struggled to find the right words. "There is just not a good way to say this, Chris, and I am going to apologize before I tell you. After this, you might not want to see me again."

An alarmed Chris knelt next to her and took her hands in his. "Mimina, what is it? Are you and your family leaving? I was afraid of that, but it is your right to choose. You are free now. I had hoped you would want to stay. My father is going to pay you a settlement, you know? I was going to come to all of you today to tell you the news. He sent the papers yesterday."

"Chris, let me talk. It has nothing to do with money. And our family is not going to accept any settlement either. You confessed to the wrongdoings of your family and I want to confess to my wrongdo-ings."

"You don't need to confess to me, Mimina. Talk with God and that is enough," a frightened Chris answered.

"It wouldn't have been enough for me if you had confessed to God that I am a free person without telling me, Chris. I thank you for finally telling us. I know it was the hardest thing in the world for you to do. I know you love your father and it will be difficult to live with him after this. Please talk with the Domi and ask him to help you. We talked with Ruben yesterday and that is why I feel I need to come clean. I want to tell my story."

Mimina shook her hands free, lowered her head, and continued. "When you were married with *Mefrou* Amy, I knew that you wanted a baby with her. I was jealous of her. I didn't want her to have a free white baby. You would love him more than my black sons. So every day, I gave your wife black bark tea to drink so she could not get pregnant. It was my fault she never conceived when you were living on this plantation."

Chris jumped up. "What?"

"I wanted to have your children. I wanted to let you feel what it was to be a slave. Your own children were slaves now. It was my way of getting back at Miriam, at you, and your family."

Chris shuddered. "I have always loved you, Mimina, always. You were the most important person in my life. How could you do this to me, to us? Because of you, I don't have any children now, not with my wife and not with you. I always have treated you well, you and your family, and now you are telling me you are guilty of this? How could you? How could you?"

While he was talking, he shuddered and took two steps back from Mimina.

Suddenly, rage rose up and once again filled Mimina's heart. "Guilty? Guilty? Do not talk to me about guilt. Any other slave in my situation would have done black magic on your wife; I only gave her some tea to drink. You and your people have misused us for generations. You owned us, for heaven's sake. Do not come to me now with a halo of light circling over your head. You are no angel yourself. If you loved *Mefrou* Amy so much, why did you keep me on the side? And what does it mean to treat a slave well? Why would you think we should treat you well? Just because of the grains of corn you threw to us from time to time?"

Mimina's eyes were spewing fire. She was mad beyond all logic, beyond all planning. "Your family got a good deal with us. First you got three medicine women for free and then you could misuse us day after day, making us believe we were slaves and putting us to work. Do you have any idea what it means to be a slave? To be the sole property of somebody else?"

"Mimina, I might not have been a slave myself but I know our family treated yours well. You had food to eat, you were not beaten or mistreated," Chris said, repeating his father's words.

"That makes you feel proud? You are a good master? You believe you are a good person because you treat us well? I have news for you—you are still a master who goes to sleep at night knowing that he owns people against their will. Do you still believe you are so good? People in 'good' masters' homes abused my family and produced children to be slaves for the family. It would have been 'good' to set the children free, but no, the 'good' masters used those children of abuse to have free slaves. Don't kid yourself, Chris. You are as bad a master as any other master."

Mimina was steaming.

"Mimina, what you are saying is not fair. I know that slavery is wrong. I have written many letters to the governor. I have been in many meetings to work toward the abolition of slavery. And you know it."

"So? If you know slavery is bad, why do you still own people? Why not set them free and pay them for their work? Don't you know black people feel the same as white people do?" Mimina insisted.

"You are trying to rationalize what you have done to me and my wife. You will not get away with it, Mimina. I don't know how you could have done it for years. Depriving me of children. I would have been a good father."

"Yes, you would have been a good father if your children were white. But with your three black children you have not been a good father. You had three sons. They lived in the same house, even though they had to use the back door and the back stairs so they would never bump into any white people. Don't you dare ask me 'how could you do this?' I am asking you, how could you live with your sons and never see them, never hug them, never talk to them man to man, year after year? Until I sent them away to try to help them become free men? At the time I was doing these things, I didn't know better. I was hurt; your sister treated me like dirt. I was beaten every day for things I did or didn't do. I hated you all back then."

After that, there was a long silence.

Mimina tried to get her anger under control. Chris was looking off into space. Finally, he said, "Mimina, you are right, I am as bad as the next master. I will not be the one throwing the first stone..."

Chris could not finish talking.

Mimina jumped up at the last words: "the first stone." The words of the Lord hit her in the face. Exactly what God didn't want her to do, she was doing: accusing Chris of his wrongdoings instead of confessing her wrongs.

"God forgive me, forgive me. Chris, forgive me, I was played by the devil. I am so sorry for what I did. I am a bad person. At least you were raised to believe the way you treated the slaves was right. I was raised better. May Yeye, Mai Sila, and Mai Didi are all women of faith. I knew better, but I let spite embitter my heart."

They both sat face down, tears streaming. Chris pushed a big yellow envelope in her direction. She took it.

Slowly Mimina stood up and left the porch quietly. Chris let her go.

The medicine women sat down and had a good talk. Mimina came clean and her mother and grand-mother prayed for her. They all felt that it was time to make big decisions.

"What were they going to do with their lives now? Fito is still a slave," Mai Sila said. "I wouldn't want to move from Master Moron's townhouse and leave him."

Mimina opened the big yellow envelope Chris gave her and was reading the papers. She showed her family the papers.

"Official documents to prove our names and our freedom," she said, and for a moment, they all were excited. She turned the papers over and said, "Mai Sila, you don't need to worry about Fito. Master Moron offered to free him also if he promises to keep doing the job he is doing now for payment. And you can keep doing your job too. You are gonna be paid for it now."

"Mai Didi, you and I can receive a large amount of money as compensation for all the work we have done in the past. And we can keep doing the work we have done in the past and receive payments. What do you think?" Mimina asked.

Mai Didi was pensive for a moment, and then she said, "I wouldn't mind staying on this plantation. I know the work, and Master Chris is a good master. He is easy to work with. But for a fresh start, I would say let's move. I think I would like to live in Pun-da, not far from Mai Sila, so we can see each other again."

Mimina had not expected her mother to dare to move, and all the way to Punda, of all places. But there it was.

"So Punda it is," she said. "We can start looking for a house. We will need money to rent a house though. And we don't have any. We have given all our money away."

"Master Moron said he wants to give us all that money, so why not take it? We worked for it, didn't we?" suggested Mai Didi.

"Ahhh... I am not sure," Mimina thought out loud. "To me it feels like blood money. Why not trust God and just get started with what we have? It would be a clean break with the master's family. They did us wrong, and we did them wrong (or I did anyway), so let's just go ahead and start by ourselves."

"Mai Didi never did anything wrong for the Master," Mai Sila protested. "She deserves to get her money."

"Yes, that is true," Mai Didi offered, "but I don't want it. If it makes Mimina feel better for us to start over new, we will do it. I am so happy that we are free and healthy and that all of us are serving the Lord. Mai Yeye would have been proud of us."

Slowly, Fito stood up and took something out of a bag. In his calm way, he commanded attention as always. All eyes were on him.

"Ahem... I was thinking, since I will be free I will not need the money I saved from selling alpargatas in the market. I was hoping to buy the freedom for

Sila and me, but I see God gave us the freedom for free, so I want to give you this money. You can use it to get started in a new house, buy material to make more soap and oil, and sell it in the market."

A completely surprised family hugged him and accepted the money with the promise to pay it back. When Mimina opened the bag, she found a total of 200 dollars! She felt rich!

Quickly they sent for Shon Pai and he went for them to Punda to find a small rental house. Shon Pai knew all the neighborhoods where free blacks lived. Even so, it was difficult to find. He spent days walking from one neighborhood to another. There were just not enough houses for free blacks, and what was available was worse than the slave huts.

Finally, he came back with some news. He was very apologetic about the house. When Mimina saw the house for the first time, she understood why. It was a small wooden building with two small bedrooms and a very small sitting room. One wall of the sitting room doubled as a kitchen.

The openings originally made for windows were closed by big pieces of old wood. It was dark and dirty inside. The doors were broken and there were no slots on the doors. There was no water and no street. The dirt road coiled among the many houses, which were built without order or planning.

Shon Pai proved himself to be a good friend. He brought four other free black men with him, and together they attacked the house. With a little of the money, Mimina bought wood and paint. Fito came to help, and in a week the house had doors and windows, four chairs and a table. The women made two mattresses, and in one of the small bedrooms they made a big table. That would become the room they would use to produce and store what they wanted to sell in the market.

Mimina gave Shon Pai one dollar but he hesitated to receive it.

"I have received so much from you, I cannot take money for this work. It was really nothing."

Mimina said, "Please take it to buy some fruit for your granddaughter. She needs it."

The very next day the women moved in. They started making oil, soap, medicine pouches, and ointment. Mai Didi thought she would like to have her own stand in the market so she could sell her products there. She was not used to handling money, but Shon Pai proved worthy again. He kept showing her until she understood how to make change. He came to Punda on market days and went with Didi to the market. He brought his own products along and she sold them for him, making a better profit for him and his family.

On some days he brought his young granddaughter, Abassi, with him and she worked along them. She had no place to stay, since Shon Pai's mother died.

Mimina made friends with Abassi, and she became like a little sister in the family. When the girl saw Mimina reading a sheet of paper she gasped.

"You can read? I wish I could. I am sure I could write all the things down that Pai makes."

Mimina was more than happy to teach her the alphabet.

Chapter Twenty Nine

It was a whole new world for the women. Mai Didi and Mimina learned to live like free people. They could sleep in now that there was no *Mefrou* or Master to be served. But habits of a lifetime were hard to break, so they rose at four o'clock anyway and went to work. Now they could leave all the dishes in the sink to be done later, but again, their little kitchen was always shining.

Mimina always wanted to have a flowery cotton dress. And now she could buy one, but she didn't. They made enough in the market. It was just the two of them, but Mimina's work as medicine women brought them in contact with many families with urgent needs. How could she justify buying such a fancy dress if her neighbors were dying for lack of a piece of bread?

They heard little news from the plantation and their old life. Mai Didi sent Fito with bottles of coconut oil, soap, and coins for her friends when business was good. Fito brought back produce like corn and watermelon for Mai Didi. Other than that, it was as if life on the plantation didn't exist.

Fito told them Master Chris was not on the island. He left shortly after the women left for a vacation in America.

Mimina thought about Chris a lot. "He wanted to take me and get married in America," she thought, her heart heavy. With a sigh, she turned her attention back to her medicine bags. This was real life: streets full of sick children, dirt everywhere, insects in and around the houses. She was needed here.

A year flew by swiftly as the medicine women continued their various ministries.

Some slaves managed to visit Mimina and asked her to help them to escape. "Don't do it," she urged them. "You will be free soon. Stay put. God will help you through."

She shared with them her own experience and how she never had seen her sons again; how she lived in daily prayer for them and hoped against hope that they would be safe wherever they were.

Some slaves were so tired of their daily situation of abuse that they decided to escape anyway. Most masters didn't send dogs after them anymore. Some masters bribed them now to come back. Masters wanted to have as many slaves as possible, hoping to collect government money for each one when abolition went through.

Mimina tried to alleviate the pain the run-away slaves had when they found her. She gave them nourishing cooked food. She helped them get cleaned up and get fresh clothes, and she prayed for them. Most of them had lots of talismans and various mixtures of belief in gods and in the African rituals. She told them about the Living God and how He sent his Son to die for all men. Many of them didn't want to embrace the white man's religion, but Mimina helped them anyway.

On their second anniversary of living independently, two things happened.

First, Shon Pai asked Mai Didi to marry him. He figured that they still had a lot of life ahead of them and why not spend it together?

Mai Didi was embarrassed to tell her family. Here she was, mother of a grown woman and seeking marriage? Two old people together? Under the guidance of Mai Sila and Mimina, Mai Didi accepted the offer and the wedding plans were made.

Later that day Fito spoke in his lazy way. "The Master came back from America this week. He asked if you all could come to the plantation. He has something urgent to tell you."

"The boys!" screamed Mimina. "He has news of the boys. Let's go."

But it was too late at night to travel, and Fito had to ask permission from Master Moron for the private use of his carriage and horse.

With sweating hands and fast-beating hearts, they approached the plantation the next day. Out of habit, they knocked on the back kitchen door.

A grinning Ruby opened it for them. In a couple of minutes the kitchen in the Big House was filled with friends and prayer group members, all laughing and talking at the same time.

The medicine women looked around at the place where they had lived their whole lives. Here they had worked from morning till evening, caring for people in the Big House. And now they were back. Their friends treated them with reverence as if they were important people and not just Mai Sila, Mai Didi, and Mimina.

Ruby ushered them quickly to the porch. For the first time in their lives, Mai Sila and Mai Didi were treated as guests on the plantation. Ruby served them a glass of lemonade. They sat in the same nice chairs that they had cleaned for so many years.

Fito was also with them. He stood behind his wife, ready to protect her. Kela, Ruby's sister, went around with little chicken sandwiches. Her face was sullen, her attitude harsh. Mai Didi took her hand in hers.

"Child, hang on. It will not be long. Always remember the One that died for us on the cross. He will fight for you with a flaming sword. Don't give up now."

Kela looked embarrassed. Was it so obvious that she was jealous of the freedom the others had received while she still took care of this big house and the kitchen?

Master Chris came onto the porch and cleared his throat. "Ahem," to get their attention.

Mai Didi felt like giving him a hug. He was her "boy," whatever happened.

Mimina's feelings were similar. She was so glad to see him again. Master Chris walked over to her and took both of her hands. He held them tenderly.

"My sisters," he addressed them, "I sent for you because I have great news. I have located the boys." He couldn't take his eyes away from Mimina.

It took a second for Mimina to understand. She looked over at her family. They also had blank faces. Then the three of them jumped up and started screaming.

"Aiiiiiiiiii, the boys? Robby, Jaques, and Ronny?"

"Are they okay?"

"Where are they?"

"Are they coming back?"

"What happened to them?"

They fired all these questions at Master Chris, while Mimina fell to her knees, laughing through her tears.

"The boys are well," said Master Chris. "They will arrive on Curacao next week. They are on a ship, *The Clermont*, coming from New York. I bought them."

Silence...

"You bought them?" Mai Sila dared to ask.

"Yes, I bought them in the USA,"

Chris repeated.

"The USA?" Nobody could believe that.

"Yes, the USA. When I hired my third investigator, he suggested I look elsewhere since he was quite sure the boys were not in Venezuela. He suggested we investigate on this island since he thought the boys were sold here and were held as slaves somewhere. He made a thorough search on all the major plantations, but he could not find them. Three handsome, light-skinned, well-educated boys who spoke more than one language could not be bought or sold here without a trace. Somebody would have found it out. So we looked farther, and the investigator checked the ship records. In the same year and month as the boys left, there was one ship in the dock, *The Columbus,* a renowned slave ship. We traveled to the USA and managed to find the captain of that ship. He remembered the boys very well. 'Never seen such well-behaved slaves before,' he said. He helped us find the first master who bought the boys. And through him we found out where the boys were located."

Mimina and her family hugged each other during the telling.

"But you saw the boys? Are they well? You sure?"

"We traveled for weeks in a stage to find the city where the boys lived. They were working in Vermont, deep inside the USA. Yes, I saw them. They look healthy and strong. They were working in the cocoa industry. They couldn't believe their eyes when they saw me. They believe I am an answer to prayer. They tried so hard to communicate with you. Robby said he had written numerous letters and asked escaping slaves or people who passed through to mail them to you, but as we know, they never arrived," Master Chris explained.

"Were they well treated?" Mimina was afraid to ask.

"They were working in a very large plantation with a cocoa factory out in the country. Their master was a harsh man and their Fito was hard to please. But somehow the boys made a name for themselves, and they told me they were treated well and ate enough. There was no room for anything else than work, though. They never saw other people and they worked long hours."

"If the boys are well, why didn't you bring them with you?" Mai Sila asked, still skeptical.

"Their Fito didn't want to sell them. They were his right-hand men and he didn't want to run the company without them." Master Chris was clearly proud of his sons.

"I had to travel again to find the owner of the company and explain to him that the boys were not slaves but my sons." He looked over at Mimina to see her reaction to this statement. It was the first time that he had acknowledged that fact in public.

"Grudgingly, the owner permitted me to buy the boys back, to avoid the lawsuit I was going to start. I bought the boys and brought them with me to New York. I could not bring them on my ship since there was no room on board. But I left the investigator with them and they will arrive next week. In the meantime, I want to prepare for them."

Didi rushed to Master Chris and hugged him tightly, just as she had when he was a young boy. She was overcome by her emotions and could not speak. Sila, Mimina, and Fito held on to each other.

"Thank you, Chris, thank you. God bless you for what you did for us. You found my sons for me. Thank you." Mimina walked slowly to Chris and hugged him close.

Later that day the prayer group was assembled and Mimina shared the good news. Everybody was clapping and laughing.

Master Chris invited the women to stay on the plantation, this time as guests in the Big House. Didi and Mimina slept in the boys' former rooms. Fito and Mai Sila were shown to a guest room. The house that had brought the women so much sorrow and backbreaking toil over the years now was a place of celebration.

"Mai," Mimina said when they were preparing for bed. "There is something I don't know how we are going to do. Chris bought the boys, so they are his slaves. This time he has a paper to prove it. We are free people now. Where are the boys gonna live?"

Slowly Mai Didi nodded. "I haven't thought about it yet. I was just too happy the boys are well. The boys were not slaves in the first place. They were stolen and sold to that slave ship."

"That is true, Mai, but Master Chris did pay for them and he has a bill of sale to prove it. They are his now."

"Yes, I guess we will need to buy them back or at least reimburse him for the trip, boat, hotel, and so on. It will take some time but we will manage. Keep the faith. Let's pray."

That very next day the problem was brought to a solution. Master Chris called them in and offered to rebuild the small house on the north side of the plantation where the tutor used to live. He thought it should be easy to build two rooms and put in new windows. "Maybe we need to repair the roof," he added. "I hope you will consider coming back and living on the plantation as free people, serving as medicine women or whatever we need. I will pay you, of course." He looked pointedly at Mimina, holding his breath.

She nodded.

And he smiled, relieved.

Everybody pitched in to repair the house. Fito, who went to Punda and brought back Shon Pai and his granddaughter, worked on the house too. Mai Didi and Mimina went to Punda and packed their personal belongings, giving away all they could to their former neighbors.

Master Chris gave permission to move the boys' beds and desks to their new house, which was looking better and better.

Mimina saw Chris almost daily. Slowly their friendship was restored. Neither of them dared to talk about the day they had their fierce fight. Also, Mimina felt afraid to be so much in Chris' debt.

Sunday morning after church, she walked leisurely back to the Big House. Chris was on the porch having a simple breakfast and reading the newspaper.

He looked up when she approached and stretched out his hands. "Mimina, we're finally alone. Come here, I have something to tell you."

Slowly Mimina walked up to him.

"I have something to say too," she retorted. "I want to thank you, Chris, for bringing my boys back. Forgive me, forgive me for what I thought ... for what I did. I take my words back. You are a real father. Thank you for buying them back."

"I didn't buy them to make them my slaves. I bought them because that was the only way in the American justice system to have them and legally take them out of the country, because their owner was not going to let them go. They will be free men in this country. I will sign the documents and I will give them my name. They are my sons now. We already talked about it, the boys and I."

Chris held her hands and looked her into the eyes. "Mimina, I know the slave system is not a good system. I was born into it and I never thought it wrong until I grew up and got to know you better. Our family did things we cannot be proud of. You have done things you are not proud of. It was the corrupt system that made us corrupt people. We have been played, Mimina, and we didn't know it. We have been played by the devil. I realize it now. It was not you doing that horrible thing. It was you, under his power. So I have forgiven you. I don't even think about it anymore. It is under the feet of my Lord Christ. I pray and hope that you can forgive me, my family, and white people in general. It was not us. It was us under the enemy's power. We were easy prey in his hands. Who wouldn't want to have private slaves tending to all their needs 24 hours a day? We bought into the system, believing ourselves special and worthy to have slaves serving us all the time. I have repented of it. I hope you will want to stay friends with me. And maybe … maybe … one day … maybe more?"

On the plantation, Mimina started a new life in their new house. Her boys arrived, mature and strong, blessed to be back home. They all moved together into the house. Mai Didi married Shon Pai, and they built an extra room onto the house for the new couple. With her boys, Mimina enjoyed life as a free woman with free sons. Chris visited them almost daily. They got to know each other very well.

Chris went to the prayer meeting and told the slaves the good news that a date was set for the abolition of the slave laws. Every one of them would be free men! The news brought many happy faces. People started planning what they would do once they were free. Some planned to move to Banda Bou and start a compound there while they searched for their lost sons, husbands, and family members. Others planned to stay on the plantation and work for pay with Master Chris.

After the service, Mimina and Chris walked together to the top of a mountain and knelt down on their knees. They prayed together.

Down in the garden of the small house, they saw their sons working the field. They were tending to their own vegetables. Together the parents gave thanks to God.

Epilogue:

On the first day of July, 1863, the sun rose on a group of free people on the island of Curacao. Some were white; some were black. Two things they had in common—they were God's chosen people, and they were free.

Mai Yeye could not be with them on this glorious day, but it was her strong faith that brought her whole family to this place. Mai Sila, old and bent, was held by the hand by her old husband Fito. Didi and Mimina held hands. Chris stood with Shon Pai and his granddaughter. They were all on the square in front of the Catholic Cathedral, where the Catholic priest read the document declaring every slave free.

On the first of July, 1863, two hours after hearing the declaration, Master Chris asked Mimina to marry him.

Mimina accepted.

Not because of what he could do for her, but because of what God had done for them.

www.ingramcontent.com/pod-product-compliance
Lightning Source LLC
Chambersburg PA
CBHW030908120626
46554CB00001B/59